Disclaimer: The opinions presented herein are solely those of the author except where specifically noted. Nothing in the book should be construed as investment advice or guidance, as it is not intended as investment advice or guidance, nor is it offered as such. Nothing in the book should be construed as a recommendation to buy or sell any financial or physical asset. It is solely the opinion of the writer, who is not an investment professional. The publisher/author disclaims any implied warranty or applicability of the contents for any particular purpose. The publisher/author shall not be liable for any commercial or incidental damages of any kind or nature.

Copyright © 2018 Charles Hugh Smith
All global rights reserved in all media
ISBN: 978-1726668729

First edition published November 2018

Oftwominds.com
P.O. Box 4727
Berkeley, California 94704

Editor: Jill Kanter
Cover design: GFB

Pathfinding Our Destiny: Preventing the Imminent Fall of Our Democratic Republic

Charles Hugh Smith

With gratitude to Jake Yocom-Piatt and Peter Kleinhans for your unstinting financial support of my work. I dedicate this book to you.

Thank you, Gary F. Baker, Adam Taggart, Constance Basset and Jill Kanter for your assistance on the text.

Table of Contents

INTRODUCTION 1
    THE PROBLEM 1
    THE CURRENT STRATEGY 1
    THE REQUIRED STRATEGY 2

SECTION I. THE DYNAMICS OF DECAY AND COLLAPSE 4
    THE STRUCTURE OF RESILIENCE AND FRAGILITY 4
    THE CHALLENGE OF ADAPTING TO PROFOUND CHANGES AND EXTREME VARIABILITY 9
        Adapting in Nature: Natural Selection 10
        Adapting in Human Systems 10
        Case Study of Non-Linear Dynamics in Action 12
    THE LIMITS OF INSTITUTIONAL ADAPTATION 15
        Pros and Cons of Extreme Optimization 16
        Why Bailouts Fail 20
        The Problem with Centralized Hierarchies 21
    NON-LINEAR CHANGE, RESILIENCE AND COLLAPSE 23
    THE ECONOMIC SOURCES OF NON-LINEAR CRISES 26
        Energy, Finance and Resources 26
        Debt and Asset Bubbles 27
        Dependence on Growth 29
        Other Economic Costs 29
    THE SOCIAL DYNAMICS OF INSTABILITY 31
    THE CORRUPTING INFLUENCE OF AFFLUENCE 33
    THE FAILURE TO EMBRACE ADAPTATION AND NEW IDEAS 35
    THE DIMINISHING RETURNS OF COMPLEXITY 36
    LINEAR SYSTEMS AND THINKING IN A NON-LINEAR WORLD 37

SECTION II. THE RISE OF NEOFEUDALISM AND OLIGARCHY 41
    THE STRUCTURE OF NEOFEUDALISM 47
    THE LIMITS OF THE MARKET AND THE STATE 52
    THE MINDSET OF THE ELITE: DENIAL, COMPLACENCY, APPEALS TO THE PAST, FAITH IN TECHNOLOGY 53
    DEBT SERFDOM 55

SECTION III. ENERGY, CREDIT, CONSUMPTION AND INFLATION 58
    WHY INFLATION IS INEVITABLE 64

SECTION IV. THE NON-LINEAR POTENTIAL OF THE FOURTH INDUSTRIAL REVOLUTION 69

Dynamics of the Fourth Industrial Revolution 70
1. A new mode of production 70
2. New social organizational tools 71
3. Limits on growth and consumption 71
4. Profits decline in a commoditized global economy 71
5. Profits from finance and globalization have peaked and are in an S-Curve decline 71
6. Ordinary labor and capital, credentials and workers with credentials are all in over-supply 72
7. Conflicts between new and old elites 72
8. Centralization vs. localization and decentralization 72
9. The limits of old models 73
10. Asymmetry between winners and losers drives conflict between markets and democracy 73
11. Post-consumer society 73
12. Resistance to "expertise" and the power of the Managerial/Technocrat class 73
13. Protected cartels are being obsoleted 74
14. Capital/talent magnets, artificial scarcity and overcoming entrenched elites 74
15. Mass Unemployment/Underemployment 74

SECTION V. THE GEOPOLITICAL CONTEXT OF A NON-LINEAR WORLD 78

SECTION VI. THE FAILURE OF STATUS QUO RESPONSES 81
The Limits of Force 81
The Appeal of the Enlightened Dictator 82
Masking Failure with Propaganda 84
Currency Debasement 85

SECTION VII. PATHFINDING A SUSTAINABLE DESTINY 89
Beyond the Market and the State 89
The Third System: The Community Economy 94
Centralization and Monopoly Optimize Corruption 96
The Essential Role of Non-State Currency 97
The Structure of Resilience and Adaptability 98
Optimizing Goals and Values 100

DE-COHERENCE AND DEGROWTH 101
PRESCRIPTIVE GUIDELINES AND GOALS 103
SELF-RELIANCE AND SELF-SUFFICIENCY 104
OPTIMIZING AGENCY AND THE DISTRIBUTION OF INCOME, CAPITAL AND SECURITY 106
STRUCTURING ACCOUNTABILITY, TRANSPARENCY AND DEMOCRACY 107
INSTITUTIONALIZING SHARED PURPOSE VIA SERVING THE COMMON GOOD 108
CHOOSING OUR DESTINY 108

Introduction

The Problem

The United States is on the crumbling precipice between linear, orderly change and non-linear, disorderly change.

When a change in output is not proportional to the change in input, this is called a *non-linear* system. In linear change, an input of 1 that yields an output of 2 continues to yield an output of 2 until the input increases to 1.5, at which point the output increases to 3. In non-linear change, an input of 1 yields an output of 2, then an output of 4, then of 8, then of 16 and so on in a rapid snowballing. In the first case, moving 1 unit of snow clears a modest path. In the second case, moving 1 unit of snow soon unleashes an avalanche.

Our economic and political structures are optimized for linear, gradual adjustments. In the non-linear era we are now entering, this means they are effectively *designed to fail*.

To prevent the fall of United States and other democratic republics, we must radically transform the structure of our current economy and society. This requires a comprehensive strategy, what some call a National Strategy (or in previous eras, a Grand Strategy). In the past, such plans were drawn up and put into action by political elites, and millions of citizens obeyed the dictates of authority. This is the model that has been dominant not just in the modern era but for imperial eras stretching back thousands of years.

In the non-linear era just ahead, the citizens will have to lead the elites, who as always will cling to their concentrated wealth and power even as the era demands the adaptability and resilience of decentralized power and capital.

The Current Strategy

The implicit assumption underpinning America's current state-market economy is that everyone's best interests are served by a winners-take-most market built on advocating for state favors—in effect, a state-cartel system that has greatly enriched the few at the expense of the many. (The vast majority of the past decade's gains in wealth and income have flowed to the top 5%, and within that class, most of the gains have flowed to the top 0.1% of households.)

Markets only factor in real-time demand, supply and price, and ignore everything beyond this narrow calculation: lifecycle and social costs, externalities, etc. Markets have no mechanisms for pricing value that isn't based on price alone (for example, resilience, positive social roles, self-reliance, etc.) The implicit strategy of markets is to maximize personal gain, make decisions based solely on price, and ignore everything that isn't factored into price.

Everything valued by other metrics is ignored, devalued or destroyed by this strategy-of-no-strategy. Biological diversity, for example, isn't included in the price discovered by markets because markets have no mechanism for valuing biological diversity. In the logic of the market, an ecosystem that's been destroyed by profiteering is of no consequence; the market will provide a substitute for whatever is no longer available.

According to this logic, the market solution to the destruction of air quality is to sell cans of fresh air, a recent innovation in heavily polluted cities in China. That what's truly valuable has been destroyed doesn't register in the logic of winner-take-most, price-is all-that-counts markets. Those claiming markets solve all problems are willfully blind to the perverse deficiencies of markets' price discovery mechanisms.

As for lobbying the state to maximize private gains: this pay-to-play institutionalizes perverse incentives and regulatory capture, a process that's already reduced our democracy to a self-serving oligarchy.

Ill-defined *national interests* guide a foreign policy of military force and commercial interests that lacks strategic coherence, predictably leading to catastrophically misguided policies that have enriched the well-connected few at the expense of the many.

Markets and advocating for state favors are not substitutes for strategy. Markets and lobbying must be guided by incentives and goals established by an explicit strategy that serves sustainability, adaptability and the common good. Anything less dooms us to decay and collapse as non-linear storms arise and envelope the world.

The Required Strategy

To pathfind an alternative destiny, we must create new structures optimized for resilience and adaptability, not for centralized wealth and control. Rather than rely on the dysfunctional incoherence of narrow self-interest and force, we need a national strategy based on evolutionary principles and systems dynamics—i.e. a system based on an understanding of the structural differences between systems doomed to collapse and those with the flexibility to adapt successfully to non-linear disruption.

This is neither an easy subject nor a breezy read. While the basic ideas are simple, understanding how they manifest in complex systems can be challenging. It may also be difficult for many of you to embrace the disconcerting and possibly bewildering idea that the entire status quo is untenable and will disintegrate not from policy errors or poor leadership but simply as a consequence of its current structure.

[handwritten margin note: fractals separated a...]

SECTION I. The Dynamics of Decay and Collapse

In this section, we'll explore dynamics of decay and collapse, starting with the basics: the structure of organizational resilience and moving on to the sources of instability leading to collapse. Our goal is to understand how states adapt or collapse based on the resilience of their economic, political and social structures.

The Structure of Resilience and Fragility

While we're drawn to narratives that feature dramatic leaders and pivotal challenges, survival or collapse of human organizations ultimately depends not on individual leaders or specific policies but on the structure of the organization. And just like human organisms, human organizational structures have traits that manifest either resiliency or brittleness. Resilient ones adapt; brittle ones collapse. Such manifestation is *scale-invariant*, meaning it holds equally true for small groups, global corporations and/or states.

Dynamics that favor maintaining the status quo are intrinsic to all organizations. These include: 1) the structural bias for current optimization; 2) incentives for insiders to protect their positions; 3) the high costs and risks of structural changes; 4) decisions based on a past that no longer exists and 5) conserving structures that once conferred an adaptive advantage but are now maladaptive.

Simply put, it's extremely difficult for organizations to change their structure once it's been institutionalized. As a result, organizations are suited for gradual, modest changes that leave their processes and outputs intact. When survival depends on radically reorganizing these structures, organizations lack the institutional mechanisms, funding, history and skills required to do so.

In other words, rapid adaptation that puts insiders at risk is not a natural function of organizations; institutionalized resistance to systemic, risky transformations makes sense when change is gradual and incremental.

As a result, organizations that aren't specifically designed to adapt very rapidly and take risks—changing their stripes, as it were, on the fly- -*are designed to fail* when conditions switch from linear to non-linear.

Every organizational structure is optimized to function in specific conditions and produce specific outputs. This optimization might be implicit, that is, not well understood by insiders within the organization, who inherit structures whose original purpose and design may have little connection to current conditions.

In this sense optimization is akin to *specialization* in the natural world, where natural selection optimizes some species for specialization to exploit a specific niche while other species are optimized for a wider range of conditions. The narrower the specialization, the greater the vulnerability to changing conditions. The slower the rate of adaptation, the lower the odds of survival in fast-changing conditions.

Optimization can be understood as *what the organization is designed to produce* or more simply, *what the organization produces as output*. Just as species develop traits and behaviors that serve their current specialization/optimization, organizations develop structures that serve their current optimization. These include structures for decision-making, collecting information, acquiring inputs, producing outputs, distributing rewards, limiting risks and managing feedback.

The output isn't limited to the stated primary purpose; it includes a wide range of tangible and intangible secondary outputs. For example, a university's primary output is the education of its students and the issuance of diplomas. But universities also produce stable employment, and if they have the necessary structures, they may produce research and alumni networks that encourage and support new enterprises. They may also generate intangible output such as prestige.

Universities can also generate student loan debt that cripples their students.

What's actually being optimized can be quite different from the purported output. If the diploma issued by the university has lost its market value, and students graduate with little measurable learning, then the university isn't optimized for its purported purpose, education of students. It's actually optimized to benefit insiders.

This is the natural evolution of organizations with centralized *power structures*: insiders have compelling incentives to maintain their power and income at the expense of the organization's output.

Every organization has a *power structure*, a mechanism for processing inputs into outputs, distributing benefits and making decisions. It could be autocratic, hierarchical, or participatory.

These structures lend themselves to optimizing certain conditions. Once those conditions change, few organizations are able to adapt to new conditions if the adaptation requires a fundamental reordering of the power structure. Very few individuals or groups voluntarily relinquish power and income, even for the good of the organization. People cling very tenaciously to the self-serving belief that whatever changes need to be made can be done while leaving their positions and power intact.

In other words, insiders prefer to conserve the status quo rather than increase the resilience of the organization, because the costs and redistribution of power required to increase resilience come at the expense of insiders. This divergence between the needs of the organization and the incentives of insiders to maintain the status quo is ultimately fatal to the organization.

This divergence manifests as political expediency, short-term thinking, magical thinking and denial—in short, insiders are incapable of recognizing and addressing problems if taking curative action disrupts the power structure.

This inability to accept the necessity of radical change is intellectual and cultural. Rather than being flexible, versatile and seeking to promote variability within the organization to strengthen adaptive capabilities, insiders *do more of what's failing/failed.*

Culturally, the required changes may be outside the institution's behavioral norms, or so far off their radar they don't even register as possibilities, much less necessities; anyone daring to propose such changes is sacked or exiled as threats to the status quo. Such institutional culling of those willing to pursue needed changes dooms the organization, as it lacks both the structures and leadership needed to institutionalize flexibility, versatility and variability.

Developing and maintaining such structures requires an investment of resources that doesn't make sense in stable eras. Once change shifts from linear (gradual and predictable) to non-linear (unpredictable and volatile), the organization lacks the time and ability to develop these structures. It's too late.

Ironically, the very success of an organization in optimizing linear stability hampers its ability to adapt to non-linear instability. This dynamic is visible throughout history: states collapse from the heights of their greatest expansion and optimization. The very success of their status quo structures makes them highly vulnerable to collapse once conditions change, as insiders lack the capacity to see problems for which the only solution is the dissolution of their institutions and power.

All systems need feedback and what Nassim Taleb calls *skin in the game*—accountability and consequence. This is the essential structure of classic markets: customers' decisions to buy is feedback on demand and price, and suppliers provide cost and availability feedback. Enterprises that lack feedback or ignore it lose sales and are eventually forced to close their doors. *Feedback, accountability* and *consequence* are the core dynamics of markets.

Bureaucracies excel at blunting or eliminating feedback, accountability and consequence. Why risk negative consequences if the organization enables avoidance of accountability and consequence?

If we combine these factors, we understand why so few organizations (and states, which are simply large organizations) are resilient when linear, predictable stability is replaced by non-linear, rapid change: they lack the structures needed to counter the intrinsic brittleness of organizations that optimize avoidance of accountability and consequence. In effect, the vast majority of institutions are optimized to *do more of what's failed*.

It is particularly difficult to accept that structures that once conferred an adaptive advantage are now maladaptive. Paolo Rognini has proposed an evolutionary dynamic which he terms *Vestigial Drifting Drives*, "the natural propensity to maintain behavior far beyond the time when the triggering motivation has been removed." This propensity also manifests in organizations as extreme resistance to the realization that all the processes that have been optimized for decades to produce a specific output—a structure and output considered highly advantageous—are not just no longer beneficial but now are in fact active hindrances to desperately needed adaptations.

We can imagine a university, for example, that appoints a committee to study how the university might adapt to the rapidly changing economy. What are the odds that the committee will conclude that virtually all the university's structures and processes are now maladaptive and must be scrapped and replaced?

We can now understand why apparently robust states collapse with such regularity: their institutions (and the state itself) were optimized for a period of linear stability insiders assumed was permanent, and so flexibility, versatility and variability were weeded out as unnecessarily costly and disruptive. As a result, core institutions lacked the structures that optimized rapid adaptation.

The ingrained bias within organizations is to conserve whatever worked well in the past, including the existing power structure. As non-linear change overwhelms the organization, those in power will sacrifice the organization itself, perhaps unwittingly, rather than see their power diminished. From the perspective of those in power, their control is the glue holding the institution together. The possibility that the power structure is itself the cause of the institution's failure simply doesn't compute.

Even if well-meaning leaders are willing to sacrifice their personal power, large institutions lack triggers that would signal the need for radical reorganization. In small businesses, the triggers are falling sales and profits. Owners who ignore these triggers are soon driven out of business. While these signals also raise alarms within institutions, large organizations have the resources to paper over warning signs. Institutional maladaptation is gradual; insiders respond to declining output by moving the goalposts (i.e. the definition of success) and making window-dressing changes to how expenses are accounted.

Institutions are also prone to *Vestigial Drifting Drives* that no longer offer selective advantages. For example, publicly funded institutions are programmed to respond to cuts in their budget as existential threats that demand the equivalent of war. Devoting resources to defend the budget made sense in flush times, but it is maladaptive when the institution's output is clearly falling and public funding is tightening across the board. The resources squandered on a losing battle to maintain funding would have been better spent on radically remaking the entire institution to become flexible, resourceful and adaptive.

The typical organization lacks the structure, history and leadership to upend a dysfunctional power structure and shift resources from well-understood processes to new and untried processes. And so the organization *does more of what's failed*, pushing whatever it has optimized as the solution, even when the problem cannot possibly be solved by the structures and processes of the past.

What organization will invest resources during stable times to maintain what appears to be an unproductive waste of time and effort, i.e. versatility and flexibility? Why create structures that have the potential to disrupt the status quo? Insiders have no vested interest in supporting institutional structures that could someday diminish their power and perquisites. Rather, they have every incentive to ruthlessly eliminate such structures to preserve the status quo that serves their interests so well.

Unlike the resilience embedded in genetic and epigenetic codes, it's costly to maintain the structures of rapid adaptability in human organizations. Why would any organization make the sacrifices necessary to maintain these capabilities if the need for them isn't even currently there?

The only exceptions are organizations that must adapt rapidly to survive—a common example being small businesses in rapidly evolving fields. To survive, these enterprises may have to change not just their product line, but their location and their organizational structure. They may not even be in the same business a few years hence. To avoid perishing, these organizations must overcome all the non-linear dynamics that arise not because of poor leadership, poor policies or ideology; rather, they arise from the very structure of the organization itself.

The Challenge of Adapting to Profound Changes and Extreme Variability

The dynamics of natural selection are not limited to organisms; human systems also conserve traits that aid survival. The core survival trait is *adaptability*, the innate ability to generate variations as the species comes under pressure, and propagate those variations that enable the species to adapt to new realities. Adaptability is scale-invariant, meaning that it's true for individuals, species, organizations and societies. The traits of *flexibility, versatility* and *variability* are the key dynamics of adaptability and thus of survival.

Adaptation/evolution is complex. It's a fool's game to predict which specific traits will prove beneficial in a new environment. Those organisms or organizations that optimize a narrow band of specific capabilities at the cost of versatility can be driven to extinction by even modest changes in their environment. Optimally, organisms and organizations must find a way to both adapt to gradual, long-term changes in their environment and also survive sudden variability that exceeds the normal range—for example, extremes of drought, heat, financial crises, war, etc.

But optimizing for gradual changes vs. optimizing for sudden extremes require different capabilities.

Adapting in Nature: Natural Selection

Many traits are conserved to serve the normal or preferred environment of the species. For example, a bird's beak lengthens to enable it to feed on long-stemmed flowers that are abundant in its habitat. But other traits must also be conserved to meet the most challenging conditions the species might face. These traits will only reveal their value in extreme conditions where the habitat is disrupted by highly variable conditions.

This critical aspect of adaptability is known as *variability selection*, the conservation of traits that favor versatility and flexibility, traits which enable species to survive fast-changing, highly variable conditions.

In other words, adaptability includes selecting traits that enable the species to adapt to gradually changing conditions (for example, rising temperatures) and the ability to survive short-term fluctuations that disrupt the normal environment.

Natural selection conserves these versatility traits via genetic/epigenetic instructions. This is how natural selection works: the survivors of extremes of drought, hunger, etc. conserve whatever genetic variations enabled their survival. Natural selection is feedback, accountability and consequence. As conditions change, the organism responds to the limit of its genetic capacity, and either survives and expires. The survivors pass on the coding for the mix of traits that enabled their survival.

Genetic/epigenetic coding is a cheap form of insurance. It doesn't cost the organism much to conserve instructions for rarely needed but essential-to-survival versatility.

Adapting in Human Systems

Human systems are not so fortunate. In human systems/organizations, the ability to survive extreme fluctuations must be consciously developed and maintained. Maintaining flexibility is not free; there are costs to maintaining this adaptability, and in times of stability, these costs appear to be superfluous.

One example is redundancy, the maintenance of spare capabilities. Carrying a spare camp stove while backpacking, for example, may seem like needless extra weight as long as the primary camp stove is functioning, but should the primary stove fail, it suddenly seems brilliant to have packed the auxiliary stove.

Some forms of redundancy are cheap, for example, buying a spare wrench to have on hand should the primary tool break. But others that require testing and maintenance are costly. The higher the cost of redundancy, the greater the skepticism in periods of stability as to its value.

Another example is a buffer. Let's say a bank maintains 5% of its deposits as reserves to cover depositors' withdrawing their money. This buffer is adequate during periods of relative stability, but should a financial panic trigger a widespread urgency to withdraw cash from banks, the bank's buffer will quickly be expended and the bank declared insolvent.

A more conservatively managed bank might maintain a buffer of 10%, and as a result it survives the panic, but only at the cost of forgoing the profits that could have been earned by lending out that additional 5% buffer.

A third example is versatility. If a construction-related problem arises and the full extent of the situation is unknown or ambiguous, does the manager dispatch four workers who each know only one trade, or is there one versatile worker who has all four skills who can be sent out?

A fourth example is dissent, variations that challenge the narratives and assumptions of the status quo. This includes skeptical inquiry, the introduction of new ideas and experimentation.

You see the point: flexibility requires tradeoffs and costs. Redundancy, buffers and versatility aren't free to develop or maintain. The default inclination of any organization that's optimized to protect the security of insiders is to repress any dissent as dangerous, and punish or exile the dissenters.

The typical approach in human systems is to weigh the risks of some extreme variation occurring and devise a buffer whose costs align with the risk (high or low). For example, if the risks of flooding are high, spending money on high flood barriers makes financial sense, as the damage from repeated flooding is costly. If the costly barriers limit the occasional extreme flooding for decades, the barriers yielded a great return on investment. Conversely, if it's decided that building barriers against 100-year floods makes little financial sense, and then there are multiple extreme floods in the span of a few years, the assessment of risk and cost will change very quickly: skimping on barriers ended up costing much more in flood damage than building barriers.

Resiliency—the ability to adapt to both gradual changes and extreme fluctuations—isn't quick or cheap to develop. And in many cases, there is the additional factor of institutional or cultural resistance to investing in what's perceived as unnecessary or even counterproductive.

Case Study of Non-Linear Dynamics in Action

War and combat offer insightful case studies of non-linear dynamics in action.

The pivotal Battle of Midway in the Pacific Theater of World War II hinged not just on leadership decisions and strategies but on often-overlooked systems of damage control, the institutionalized capability to survive the most challenging sea-based combat conditions: multiple hits from torpedoes and bombs, onboard fires fed by fuel and munitions, etc.

The Japanese Navy optimized an idealized strategy in which their ships suffered little damage while destroying opposing forces with offensive capabilities. As a result, there was very little institutional infrastructure for damage control training or equipment. Culturally, damage control was viewed as defeatist.

Ironically, Japan's loss of their four aircraft carriers in the battle of Midway to U.S. Navy dive bombers—the cream of the Imperial Fleet, and a blow they never recovered from—was due in part to this institutional choice to optimize offensive capabilities and discount damage control as defeatist.

In contrast, damage control was an integral part of U.S. Navy training and shipboard infrastructure.

Thus when Japanese pilots left the U.S. aircraft carrier *Yorktown* in flames and listing badly, dead in the water, they reported the carrier as lost. But onboard damage control efforts extinguished the fires and got the ship underway again, much to the surprise of the Japanese. When the *Yorktown* was later sighted steaming under its own power, no longer trailing plumes of smoke, Japanese observers assumed it was a newly arrived aircraft carrier that was just joining the battle.

The point here is that organizations have a choice that few clearly discern: resources can be invested in optimizing the preferred or idealized environment, or they can be invested in capabilities that appear to have little value until conditions become extremely challenging, i.e. non-linear. Those who presume such conditions will never arise, or over-estimate the resilience of their systems, belatedly discover their presumption leads to disaster.

To recap, using the pivotal carrier-based battle as an example: every blue-water navy had to adapt to the profound change in naval strategy from relying on surface warships to air power based on aircraft carriers. Those who failed to adapt were destroyed in the first contact between their surface ships and carrier-based air power.

But this was not the only essential adaptation: navies also had to evolve an ability to operate carrier battle groups that integrated surface ships and submarines to protect the carriers. In other words, developing the offensive capacity of aircraft carriers was only half of what was required to survive combat; navies also had to develop defensive capacities to protect their carriers from enemy attacks.

As well, navies that developed flexible carrier group capabilities had a greater range of options in the highly non-linear environment of warfare. If a rigidly organized (i.e. optimized for specific scenarios, highly centralized, intolerant of dissent) naval force meets an opposing force that is more versatile and has a greater capacity to survive non-linear conditions (i.e. optimized for flexibility), the rigidly organized force may prevail if the conditions of battle align with its idealized optimization.

But if conditions change rapidly or veer outside the optimized scenario, the more flexible force is likely to carry the day, even if it has fewer assets.

This brief analysis helps us understand why apparently robust states collapse in crisis: they appeared robust in normal conditions because their institutions were optimized for a narrow range of stable conditions they reckoned was permanent.

But stability is never permanent; things change, and often generate feedback loops that strengthen the destabilizing effects of what at first glance looked like a minor problem. This is the essence of a non-linear system: multiple feedback loops interact in difficult-to-forecast ways.

Returning to our example of damage control and the Battle of Midway: The true cost of leaving their aviation fuel lines exposed was only revealed to the Japanese leadership when all four of their aircraft carriers had been reduced to infernos by relatively few hits—in one case, a single bomb destroyed the entire carrier by igniting fires that could not be controlled once aviation fuel and munitions were ignited.

Those focused on optimizing offensive combat operations were blind to the costs of under-investing in the capability to survive extreme challenges. And even if they realized the true cost of discounting damage control and sought to fix this deficiency, there was no easy or cheap way to distribute the needed infrastructure, training and culture throughout a fleet that was steeped in tradition and orthodoxy—an organization that was intolerant of dissent.

Those who suppress dissent as a danger to the status quo are in effect eliminating a key component of adaptability and resilience: the unpredictable variability of individuals' insights and questions.

Developing institutional knowledge and infrastructure takes more than just investment, time and training; it requires replacing the previous mindset and slowly nurturing a new one that requires not just the nuts and bolts of new equipment and training but an institutionalized openness to dissent.

Author/analyst Donella Meadows explained that changing systems requires adding new feedback loops; adjusting existing parameters won't change the system. We can add that accountability and consequence must also be present to make use of the new feedback.

Adding a new feedback loop sounds innocuous, but that apparently benign process has the potential to disrupt power structures. How many organizations have the capacity to add new feedback loops and the will to accept the risk that this might disrupt the status quo?

In other words, versatility and flexibility in service of adaptability require a suite of capabilities that can take the operational equivalent of genetic instructions and add feedback loops that distribute and refine new variations rapidly.

Very few institutions have the capability, will or means to throw off their own organizational and cultural dysfunction. As a general rule, organizations expire long before they develop the requisite capabilities and culture needed for rapid adaptation. The cumbersome processes and glacial timelines that function in periods of stability are fatal in eras of non-linear change.

A national strategy that doesn't understand the organizational limits of adaptability will fail in a spectacularly unexpected fashion. Assuming that optimizing the present stability will be successful because this stability will endure into the indefinite future is a well-trod path to collapse.

The Limits of Institutional Adaptation

Institutions conserve what worked in the past, and their bias is to project a linear continuation of current trends. Given that the institution is structured to optimize these trends, the leadership naturally predicts the organization can handle any future challenges.

But if the future is not a linear continuation of existing trends but a non-linear fracturing of these trends, then institutions optimized for linear stability may be the *wrong structure* and the *wrong unit size*, to borrow a phrase from author Peter Drucker.

The choice of what kind of resiliency one invests in is only part of the story. The other part is the resilience or brittleness intrinsic to organizational structures themselves. When conditions change, a structure that worked well in current conditions may fail not from poor leadership or bad policies, but as a result of the limits of the organization's structure.

For example, in choosing centralized structures we are choosing to optimize decision-making that's concentrated in the hands of a few at the top of the power pyramid. Centralized hierarchical organizations such as governments and large corporations are the dominant structures of our economy and society. Given the ubiquity and historical success of this type of organization, it's easy to overlook that we're accepting a trade-off in making this the default organizational type: this structure, so successful at organizing people and capital, is vulnerable to failure when centralization itself becomes the problem.

The success of highly optimized centralized organizations masks the limitations of centralization.

Pros and Cons of Extreme Optimization

Consider Apple, recently lauded (in mid-2018) as the first American-based company with a $1 trillion market capitalization. Apple optimizes very specific conditions: 1) an extremely limited number of consumer products and services sold globally; 2) total control of the supply chain, marketing, distribution and retailing; 3) tight integration of software and hardware; 4) obsessive attention to design and functionality of the products and 5) careful management of the brand to optimize its uniqueness.

Feedback, accountability and consequence are in the company's DNA. In a consumer-driven global economy that places a premium on status, Apple's optimization has yielded stellar financial returns.

But how much of this kind of highly centralized optimization can be applied to non-consumer areas of human endeavor? Is this model of centralized control pursuing extreme optimization successful everywhere it's used, or is its success limited to specific conditions?

Optimization can itself be a weakness, as this is the structural equivalent of *monoculture*: optimizing output by growing one crop and eradicating all insect pests, competing plants, etc. Monocultures are linear systems, and as long as nothing non-linear occurs, it seems like the maximal productive structure.

But non-linearity is endemic, and so eventually a blight arises that is immune to herbicides, or a pest evolves resistance and the entire monoculture is wiped out.

Growing multiple varieties of the same crop might reduce the yield but increase resilience, while growing a wide range of crops as well as multiple varieties of each crop would greatly increase adaptability and versatility. Variety and variability are core dynamics of resilience and adaptability.

Should conditions change, the extraordinary rewards of extreme optimization might vanish and the institutional limits of centralized control becomes a point of failure. Going back to the example of the Imperial Japanese Navy's optimization of carrier-based air offensives: who questioned this optimization after its remarkable success at Pearl Harbor? Yet even as the victorious aircraft were landing on their carriers, the seeds of their demise were already planted in the optimization trade-offs that invested so little in damage control.

Increasing centralization has been a successful strategy for empires and enterprises for millennia, as it enables command and control of far-flung holdings and the unification of goals, resources and labor. But this concentration of power and decision-making also makes the system vulnerable to non-linear disruptions that turn centralized control into a fatal liability.

The point here is the model of highly centralized organizations optimized for specific processes work well in stable eras where conditions change incrementally. But should the speed and scale of change increase rapidly, a decentralized structure is better-suited than a centralized organization, as each part of the system can respond independently and quickly to local conditions.

Currency (state-issued money) is a centralized system as well. A central state issues its own currency and demands all its citizenry use only this currency as money. That's advantageous to the state, but not necessarily to its people, as Venezuela has recently witnessed with its destruction of the purchasing power of its currency, the bolivar. Does anyone doubt the citizenry would have been better served with a decentralized system that allowed the use of multiple competing currencies?

By their very nature, centralized organizations tend to default to a variety of fatal dysfunctions. To protect themselves from scrutiny and consequence, insiders limit transparency and accountability and suppress dissent; fiefdoms arise, and doing more of what's failed becomes the orthodoxy.

Once its charismatic leader Steve Jobs was forced out, Apple drifted to these defaults, leaving the company just 90 days from insolvency within a decade. To save the company, Jobs revolutionized its culture and structure: fiefdoms were eliminated as all divisions were melded into one unit, bloated staffing was slashed, decisions were trimmed from months to days (or even hours), management was flattened to the board of directors and a management team and the entire company was focused on a very few products and priorities.

But this sort of radical transformation of centralized organizations are rare. Institutions are programmed to cling to what no longer works, even as new dynamics emerge that the institution is ill-equipped to adapt to. No institution, or division of an institution, will voluntarily surrender its power, prestige or budget merely because it's failing.

Instead, insiders seek to protect themselves from accountability and consequence. This is the nature of institutions that conserve stability and continuity: they attract people who value stability and continuity above novelty, innovation, flexibility and variability (i.e. dissent).

Thus the people working in institutions are self-selected to favor secure jobs and rigid processes. They chose to work for a stable institution for the very reason that they are unsuited to non-linear, fast-changing (i.e. risky and insecure) environments. This self-selected cadre is incapable of dismantling the institution and sacrificing its organizational structure to adapt to fast-changing realities for two reasons: 1) the organization itself lacks the structures required, and 2) by its conservation of rigid, sclerotic processes, the institution has already weeded out anyone who favored variability over stability.

As a general rule, those who are adept at adapting to non-linear disruption soon abandon institutions due to their frustration with the hierarchical structure, the conservation of incompetence (because no one can be fired), the absence of skin in the game (where insiders continue to win awards and get pay raises even as institutional dysfunction gathers momentum), the culture of self-service (gaming the system to maximize vacation time and pensions, etc.) and the general resistance to development of the disruptive traits of adaptation.

All of the above conditions leave institutions without the resources and structures required to adapt to fast-changing, non-linear times.

In the private sector, organizations that lose the ability to adapt go bankrupt and cease to exist. Public institutions can continue doing more of what's failed until their funding collapses.

This is not the failure of the insiders, who are responding rationally to the organization's incentives, or of specific policies. The failure is coded into the very structure of centralized hierarchical organizations, which are designed to optimize stability and continuation of trend. Centralized hierarchical organizations are intrinsically unsuited to optimizing non-linear changes because there is nothing in their DNA to enforce accountability and optimize flexibility.

The incentives presented to insiders diverge from the incentives needed to serve the organization's adaptability. Incentives to sacrifice for the good of the organization are replaced with self-aggrandizement in service of maximizing private gains.

The Roman Empire offers an example. In the pre-Imperial Roman Republic, Senatorial elites were expected to serve in the front lines of the Army and pay for public buildings with their own money. As historian Peter Turchin pointed out, one-third of Rome's senatorial elite were killed in combat during the disastrous defeat of the Roman Army at Cannae. The incentives of the early Republic demanded this sort of sacrifice and skin in the game; anyone who evaded these duties and attempted to claim to power was rejected by the people and the elite. Contrast this close alignment of incentives that served both personal and organizational goals with the later Imperial era of decline during which the Roman elites sought to maximize their own private gain at the expense of the empire they claimed to serve.

Success breeds this particularly damaging form of rot. The success of institutions breeds a sense of entitlement to maximize personal gain. Since the system is presumed to be permanently successful, maximizing personal gains at the expense of the institution is implicitly incentivized: who will even notice my skimming in such a vast and powerful structure?

There is another fatal dynamic within centralized organizations. Whatever output has been optimized is like a hammer, and so everyone inside the organizations only sees nails: every problem is deemed one that the organization's hammer can solve.

This is one root source of *doing more of what's failed*. The organization optimizes a very narrow set of processes or outputs, and it's very difficult to change those optimizations due to the rigid structure, slow decision-making, self-selected risk avoidance of the leadership, and institutional conservation of what worked in the past.

The path of least resistance is to contextualize every challenge as one that can be solved by existing processes: everything becomes a nail that the organization's hammer can successfully pound down.

But *doing more of what's failed* is not adaptability, or flexibility or resilience; it merely accelerates the decay and collapse.

To ask insiders within a failing organization to understand that their organization is incapable of solving problems created by the very structure of their organization is asking the impossible. Who is willing to dismantle their livelihood and security? Should an outsider attempt radical reform, the insiders will be galvanized to defend the failing organization and their stake in it. This resistance is understandable but fatal to the organization.

There are very few Steve Jobs who can return to an organization they co-founded with enough clout to radically reorganize the power structure and lay off thousands of insiders, completely transforming processes and outputs.

Though this type of radical is the only path to survival, the typical insider will cling on to the existing system until it collapses.

Why Bailouts Fail

The other default dynamic in organizations, but especially centralized systems, is to see additional funding as the solution to the organization's failure. Rather than deal with the organization's maladaptive processes, insiders demand more money to fund *doing more of what's failed*.

Before Steve Jobs returned to save Apple from self-destruction, the company was losing over a billion dollars a year. If this had been a public-sector organization, those benefiting from the existing system would have lobbied to increase funding to cover the loss and enable doing more of what's failed.

This is why public-sector debt is soaring: the path of least resistance politically is to borrow more money to maintain maladaptive processes, since that path meets little resistance. Insiders always favor increased funding and resist any reorganization that threatens their security.

This is a variation on the dynamic mentioned above: the success of relying on debt to fund failing organizations creates a belief that there is no reason not to borrow another trillion dollars, since the economy easily digested the previous trillion-dollar increase in debt.

Debt appears linear until the system becomes non-linear, i.e. small perturbations trigger financial avalanches. The system appears stable right up to the point of failure. Beneath the surface, every additional trillion dollars of debt saps the system's resilience. Once resilience has been eroded, the debt machine collapses.

This is also an example of the divergence of incentives. Insiders are highly incentivized to borrow more money (easy, painless) rather than radically transform their failed organization (difficult, painful).

The Problem with Centralized Hierarchies

Since centralized hierarchies are the dominant organizational type in our current system, the idea that this structure, which has served so well for so long, is now the *wrong structure* and *wrong unit size*, is incomprehensible to those employed by these institutions. Unable to make this intellectual leap, they revert to humanity's protective postures of denial, rationalization and magical thinking.

Since human nature hasn't changed in a few thousand years, we find these same institutional responses in the decline of the Western Roman Empire and the Ming Dynasty in China, both of which were extremely effective in their heyday. In the decline phase of these empires, when complacency and self-aggrandizement replaced shared purpose and flexibility, insiders turned to magical thinking, claiming a return to the glory days was inevitable, as if the empire's long history of success would magically restore capabilities that had long been lost. This comforting perspective was based solely on history, not on the atrophied capabilities of the present.

The irony is that the very structure of centralized hierarchies dooms any system to collapse that suddenly needs to optimize fast adaptation. Centralized organizations are incapable of fast adaptation for all the key reasons laid out in this section: they are the *wrong structure* and *wrong unit size*, and no centralized organization will voluntarily give up its power, wealth and control when everyone in the organization is presented with powerful incentives to *keep doing more of what's failed*.

There is another self-defeating dynamic intrinsic to centralized organizations: the false sense of security created by authority. In the early stages of non-linear crisis, centralized organizations still have the wherewithal to enforce compliance to new rules. But as the crisis deepens, the cost of enforcing obedience rises, and the structure of enforcement decays.

The organization's ability to provide incentives also decays as costs rise and funding unravels. In the late stages of Imperial Roman decline, multitudes of orders were sent down the chain of command, but there was no longer an incentive to compel obedience. The system of accountability—checking on who was obeying and who wasn't—also decayed, so the stick of punishment and the carrot of reward lost their influence over those far from the center of power.

The power to enforce obedience gives the leadership a false sense of control and thus confidence that they can resolve the crisis by bending the organization to their will. But brittle, sclerotic organizations staffed with self-serving, risk-averse managers cannot be willed into a flexible, fast-responding structure. The institutional infrastructure simply doesn't exist and cannot be created on the fly, any more than Japan's Imperial Fleet could make damage control a priority with a flurry of orders.

Regardless of how leadership responds, the initial burst of obedience doesn't actually solve the core problems; it simply staves off disaster for a short time at great cost.

Obedience in centralized hierarchies is another manifestation of a central flaw in this organizational type: *it's too easy*. When it's too easy to issue commands that must be obeyed, to borrow money to paper over systemic failure, to eliminate transparency and accountability with a bureaucratic thicket of complexity—nothing new is created, nothing difficult is solved. The default pathways are trod until the path collapses into the abyss.

As a thought experiment, let's ask: if we wanted to design an organization that would appear stable in calm seas but fail once storms arise, what processes, structures and incentives would we build in? The ideal structure for guaranteeing collapse would be as follows:

- inflexible, lacking versatility
- a power structure that concentrates decision-making in a few hands who have been selected to be risk-averse and linear in their thinking
- processes that lack transparency and accountability
- diverging incentives that favor maximizing personal gains at the expense of the organization
- dependence on debt
- fierce resistance to any reorganization that trims the power or pay of insiders
- incentives for doing more of what's failed
- and so on—every trait of centralized hierarchies we've discussed in this section.

Organizations that lack adaptability—flexibility, versatility and variability—lack resilience. When slow linear change is replaced by rapid non-linear change, they have neither the structure nor the capability nor the time needed to develop resilience. Despite their apparent stability, collapse is the only possible output of brittle, maladaptive structures that optimize doing more of what's failed.

You may have noted that I haven't mentioned ideology or political affiliations in this discussion. The reason is because ideology and political affiliations play no role in the dynamics being discussed. Brittle, maladaptive structures can be communist, capitalist, autocratic, theocratic or socialist. The label attached to the regime harboring maladaptive structures has zero bearing on their vulnerability to collapse.

Non-Linear Change, Resilience and Collapse

When a change in output is not proportional to the change in input, this is called a non-linear system. An example is the famous flapping of a butterfly's wings that unleashes a distant hurricane: the output (a hurricane) is out of proportion with the input (a butterfly's wings flapping).

Nature is fundamentally non-linear, as are all complex systems. To understand how apparently stable systems can collapse quickly, let's return to the previous example of a bank panic in which depositors suddenly worry that their money isn't safe in the bank and rush to withdraw it.

Based on a linear projection of average daily withdrawals and deposits, the bank keeps 5% of its total deposits in cash as a reserve against withdrawals and losses from borrowers defaulting on loans issued by the bank. As a buffer against extreme conditions, the bank maintains a line of credit with another financial institution so it can borrow an additional 5% should the need arise.

As long as the system is linear, the bank is stable.

But then a financial panic strikes, a not uncommon, unpredictable occurrence in the financial system. As withdrawals increase, the bank reassures depositors there are sufficient funds, and activates its line of credit as a prudent reserve.

But the panic doesn't subside as expected, and soon the bank's cash and line of credit have been depleted. The bank asks for an additional loan, but the other financial institution is wary of risking any more of its capital, so it refuses.

At 10 am the next morning, a depositor withdraws the modest sum of $1,000, and the bank is declared insolvent and closes its doors. The output—the closure of the bank—is out of proportion with the input— the seemingly minor withdrawal of $1,000.

One of the factors that increases non-linearity is *hyper-coherence*, the tight links between complex systems in the global economy. In this example, a banking crisis in a distant nation might trigger a global contagion that generates such a bank run.

As explained before, the 5% cash reserve is a buffer that is designed to absorb unusual surges of withdrawals and defaults, much like wetlands buffer the storm surge from offshore hurricanes.

As buffers thin, the danger of sudden collapse increases, but the thinning of buffers is invisible to everyone but those with the knowledge and access to monitor the thinning.

For all the reasons described in the previous section, insiders tend to downplay the risk of collapse, rationalizing magical thinking and denial, in effect counting on previous stability to reassert itself. Efforts to restore the buffer tend to repeat whatever worked in the past, even if the conditions are entirely different.

In our example, let's say the bank barely survives the bank run, clinging precariously to less than 1% of remaining deposits on hand while having to pay interest on the money it borrowed in the crisis.

On the surface, the bank looks stable and everyone inside and outside the bank assumes a return to pre-crisis conditions is assured. But the distant financial crisis has disrupted various parts of the global financial system as a result of the system's *hyper-coherence*. Deposits slow, the interest on the debt taken on in the crisis eats away at the bank's earnings, and the process of rebuilding cash reserves is anemic and fitful.

The bank's buffers remain severely depleted, and so the surface stability is deceptive; the return of "calm" is only relative to the previous panic state because of the buffers not yet being fully recharged.

Then another financial arises elsewhere in the system, one that spreads a contagion to housing markets around the world. Defaults of the bank's outstanding mortgages begin to pile up, and in response the bank starts playing financial tricks to mask the defaults and keep the losses from being recorded on the bank's balance sheets. These tricks include making new loans to borrowers so they can make mortgage payments for a few more months, reducing their mortgage payments to a nominal sum, creating a new category in the balance sheet for temporarily non-compliant loans, and so on. But none of these processes actually address the real problem; they merely paper it over in the hopes that some bolt from the blue will magically bail out the defaulting borrowers and rebuild the bank's buffers.

At this point the bank could undertake a radical reorganization by closing branches and slashing management's compensation, selling off assets, seeking new deposits in underserved markets, selling impaired assets and booking the losses, and so on. But such radical actions are risky, and fearing the risk and the perception that the bank is in trouble, the management decides instead to borrow more money at high rates of interest to stabilize the situation.

But the stability is also illusory. The higher interest actually decreases the bank's buffer and increases its vulnerability to external shocks or unexpected consequences of management's decisions. Thus when a sudden spike in mortgage defaults cannot be hidden from auditors, the bank is declared insolvent.

Every action of management increased the brittleness of the organization by conserving maladaptive policies that thinned its buffers while creating a false façade of stability.

This is the global financial system in a nutshell. The average person sees stability, but beneath the surface the unprecedented expansion of debt has thinned the system's buffers and increased its hyper-coherence. The system's resilience and adaptability have been sacrificed to maintain a surface stability.

An avalanche is one example of a non-linear system. Beneath the placid surface of apparently stable snowpack, conditions are changing. At some unpredictable point, a small input causes the snow to give way in an avalanche.

Much of what we take for granted as permanently stable is actually hovering on the boundary of non-linear collapse. Many of the systems we rely on have been rescued by fortuitous discoveries of new resources or an influx of borrowed money (i.e. debt). But history informs us that relying on fortuitous discoveries and debt to save us from radical reorganization is not a sustainable strategy. Deeply destabilizing events occur on a regular if unpredictable schedule, and if systems are fragile, these events cause apparent stability to collapse with a suddenness that surprises the unwary.

The resilience of our systems is illusory. Unprecedented expansions of debt and currency have papered over the maladaptive nature of these structures. The only National Strategy with any value going forward is one that restructures systems to withstand non-linear dislocations. These are not disasters for the well-prepared—they are opportunities.

The Economic Sources of Non-Linear Crises

Energy, Finance and Resources

The global economy is dependent on three material systems: fossil fuels, finance, and natural resources (fresh water, soil, minerals, lumber, etc.—what some call *the natural economy*, as these resources are knitted together in ecosystems).

The three are deeply intertwined, as the financial sector supplies the immense sums of capital required to discover, develop and deliver fossil fuels and other resources. For example, it was recently (2018) estimated that the fracking industry in the U.S. has lost a cumulative $5 billion in the past few years of operation. This illustrates the essential role that cheap, abundant credit plays in the energy sector. Should capital become scarce and expensive, the energy sector would not be able to continue operating at current cost levels—levels that are increasingly unaffordable to consumers due to tightening global supplies of oil.

Energy has always been the master resource in civilization. In pre-industrial time, the use of draft animals (then a new energy source for agriculture), water wheels, windmills and sailing ships increased the energy sources available.

Despite the hoopla about alternative energy—wind, solar, geothermal, etc.—these only provide about 3% of global energy consumption. The global economy is still dependent on fossil fuels being abundant and affordable, and to accomplish this the energy sector must have access to abundant, cheap credit.

All three—energy, finance and resources--are non-linear systems in which minor perturbations can trigger disruptions far out of proportion to the input. This non-linearity is exaggerated by the hyper-coherence (inter-connectedness) of energy, finance and resources in the global economy. As an example, should the cost of oil rise dramatically, that quickly impacts the cost of food, which is ultimately a derivative of the cost of oil, along with oil-dependent industries such as tourism, transportation, shipping, and manufacturing.

Debt and Asset Bubbles

Our economy, society and state are now completely dependent on expanding debt and speculative bubbles, dynamics I've discussed in my previous books. As evidence of the non-linear nature and fragility of debt-based growth and speculative bubbles, recall that the Global Financial Meltdown of 2008-09 resulted from defaults in subprime home mortgages, which constituted a modest corner of the global financial system (roughly $500 billion in a global financial system of approximately $300 trillion in assets).

The implosion of subprime debt triggered a relatively minor reduction in the *rate of expansion of global credit*, and this slight perturbation in the rate of credit expansion very nearly collapsed the entire global financial system.

Central banks issued trillions of dollars of quantitative easing, guarantees, zero-interest lines of credit and other giveaways to the banking sector to save the brittle, fragile system from imploding.

The central banks' solution to this brittle fragility was to inflate another brittle, fragile simulacrum of prosperity via speculative bubbles in stocks, bonds and real estate. These bubbles have added some $30 trillion in "wealth" to U.S. households, but the non-linear nature of speculative bubbles has been masked by an unprecedented decade of central bank inflation of these assets.

Recall that central banks once lowered interest rates and offered low-cost lines of credit to banks for a few months during a recession. Now central banks have been shoveling monetary stimulus into the financial system for 10 years, including direct purchases of bonds and stocks in the trillions of dollars.

This unprecedented scale of essentially permanent intervention begs the question: what are they afraid might happen if they stopped the unprecedented stimulus? The fact that only now, at the end of a decade of stimulus, are central banks daring to take baby steps toward a less manipulated market, reveals the fragility and brittleness of a hyper-coherent global financial system that is totally dependent on accelerating credit expansion to maintain the semblance of stability.

The system's dependence on speculative asset bubbles is underappreciated by the public and the managerial elites. The basic issue is the ratio of earnings needed to service the debt (and have enough left to support the consumer spending that is the life blood of the global economy) and the total debt owed.

In the most general sense, the nation's GDP (gross domestic product) is a measure, however imperfect, of the real-world economy's ability to service debt. If GDP is stagnant and debt is rising fast, even with low interest rates, eventually consumer spending will be crimped as servicing the soaring debt absorbs more of the national income.

In 2018, U.S. GDP is about $20 trillion and total debt is $70 trillion, 3.5 times GDP. In 1992, the ratio was 2.3 (debt $15 trillion, GDP $6.5 trillion). In 2001, the ratio was 2.85 (debt $30 trillion, GDP $10.5 trillion). In 2008, at the height of the financial crisis, the ratio hit 3.7 (debt $54.6 trillion, GDP $14.7 trillion). This shows that the ratio of GDP to debt has barely improved from the crisis level of 10 year ago.

It's also useful to compare GDP with the valuations of assets: how large is the real-world economy compared to the asset bubbles being inflated on the back of the economy?

In 1981, at the start of financialization, the GDP was $3.2 trillion and net worth of households was $10 trillion—or about 3 times GDP. By 2001, it had expanded to 4 times with GDP at $10.5 trillion and net worth $40 trillion. In 2017, the GDP was $19.5 trillion and net worth was $100 trillion—5 times GDP.

In other words, the valuation of assets is expanding far faster than the real economy. In past eras of expansion, assets rose in step with the expansion of the real economy. But in the current era, assets are rising in value in lockstep with the expansion of debt rather than the real economy.

Lastly, consider the income available to purchase assets and the total value of assets: total household incomes reported to the IRS and net worth of households. In 1996, in the middle of the dot-com bull markets in stocks and a rising real estate market, total household income was $4.5 trillion and net worth was about $25 trillion—about 5.5 times total household income . In 2016, the latest data available from the IRS, household income totaled $10.2 trillion and net worth approached $100 trillion—close to 10 times household income.

By any measure or ratio one chooses, from the above data it's clear that debt and asset valuations have exploded higher and are more highly leveraged compared to the real-world economy and national income. The increase in the risk of a non-linear crisis and the system's vulnerability to such a crisis is not an opinion—it's clearly visible in the broadest measures of data.

Dependence on Growth

As for growth: the global status quo has one article of faith shared by everyone from communists to theocrats to free-market capitalists: growth is the one necessity for increasing prosperity. The idea that the planet has limited resources that are accessible at costs we can afford does not factor into this faith. The belief is that growth will overcome every obstacle and continue forever, or at least until the sun expands and burns the Earth to a crisp some billions of years in the future.

This faith in growth overlooks the inherent non-linearity of the resources required for growth: fresh water, conducive weather, fertile soil, minerals we can afford to mine and process, etc. —and on the non-linearity of debt and leverage.

Other Economic Costs

Complicating our understanding of these non-linear systems is the incompleteness of our economic models in terms of measuring *externalities* such as the systemic costs of pollution, loss of biodiversity and the second-order consequences of markets driven solely by the goal of maximizing profits by any means available. These costs are ignored in the current measures of economic activity.

Energy, finance and resources are tangible non-linear systems that we see in daily life, and so we intuitively grasp their foundational roles in the global economy. But there are also non-tangible non-linear systems that are integral to the stability of any economy: social mobility, which includes opportunities to participate in the power structure and acquire capital, and shared purpose, which is the core of *social cohesion*. When these traits are lost, the economy becomes fragile and the state is ripe for disorder and dissolution.

Though economists rely on data-centric models such as *aggregate demand* to explain the economy and finance, what's lacking is an understanding that economies are *social constructs*. Economic models appear to have explanatory value in stable eras, but as social constructs, economies are intrinsically non-linear systems prone to disorder. The narrow confines of current economic models have no conceptual tools for understanding the non-linear nature of social constructs.

Consider the dynamic of wealth and income inequality. Econometric models offer essentially zero insight into the transition when inequality shifts from being linear and non-linear. At some point, rising wealth and income inequality become non-linear, and the status quo breaks down in social disorder. Aggregate demand and similar concepts offer no predictive value or insight into the collapse of the social construct due to extreme wealth and income inequality.

Economics is equally useless in understanding how rising prices can shift from linear projections—for example, if the cost of beef is rising, people will substitute cheaper meats—to non-linear revolution and the overthrow of the state. Historian David Hackett Fischer illuminated the correlation of rising prices and social upheaval in his book *The Great Wave: Price Revolutions and the Rhythm of History*, and historian Peter Turchin has written extensively on *integrative* and *disintegrative* phases, cycles that correlate with archeological data such as coin hoards, which become common in times of disruption and conflict.

Turchin listed three conditions that characterize disintegrative phases of profound social disorder: 1) stagnating real wages, 2) the expansion of a parasitic elite class, and 3) deterioration of state finances.

These socio-economic cycles of expansion, stagnation and decline are based on rising demand for resources that are abundant and affordable in the beginning of the cycle. But by the end of the cycle, demand exceeds supply, and resources become increasingly unaffordable or unavailable at any price.

Our economy is optimized for very specific conditions of energy, finance, wages and resources: mass consumption of goods and services funded by cheap credit, rising real wages, low inflation, and cheap abundant energy and other natural resources. If any of these conditions are unavailable, the system breaks down and generates non-linear political and social discord.

When energy costs spike, recession follows as night follows day. When credit costs soar, consumption falls. When earned income stagnates as costs climb, mass consumption declines and the economy contracts.

The era of cheap abundant liquid fuels, low inflation and stable work/wages is ending. The erosion of these fundamentals has been papered over with tens of trillions of dollars in newly issued currency and credit. But issuing more currency and credit hasn't changed the fact that the easy-to-extract oil is fast-depleting, that the earnings of the bottom 90% have stagnated despite monumental stimulus, that credit costs cannot be suppressed without creating vast imbalances, and that central bank stimulus has vastly increased wealth/income/political power inequality that are unleashing non-linear political and social disruption.

We will discuss the non-linear dynamics of energy, credit, capital, labor and inflation in a later section.

The Social Dynamics of Instability

Supply-demand imbalances are not the only sources of non-linear disruptions in social constructs. As Turchin explains, the power structure of any society is not simply a hierarchical pyramid with a ruling elite at the top demanding obedience of everyone below. Turchin identified "the degree of solidarity felt between the commons and aristocracy" as a key ingredient of the Republic of Rome's enormous success. Turchin calls this attribute of social structure *vertical integration*.

In Turchin's work, *vertical integration* refers to the sense of purpose and identity shared by the top, middle and bottom of the entire wealth/power pyramid. One measure of this vertical integration is the degree of equality/inequality between the commoners and the aristocracy.

In his book *War and Peace and War: The Rise and Fall of Empires*, Turchin tells this anecdote:

"Roman historians of the later age stressed the modest way of life, even poverty of the leading citizens. For example, when Cincinnatus was summoned to be dictator, while working at the plow, he reportedly exclaimed, 'My land will not be sown this year and so we shall run the risk of not having enough to eat!'"

In other words, successful civilizations have a shared sense of purpose, what Turchin describes as a "lack of glaring barriers between the aristocracy and the commons," and a shared willingness to sacrifice in which the elites sacrifice more than the commoners for the common good.

Thus societies in which commoners can better their social and financial status are more resilient than societies that enforce servitude with little social mobility. The reason is self-explanatory but profound: if commoners have a stake in the system, they are willing to sacrifice to maintain it. But if they are oppressed by a tiny elite, the destruction of that leadership by another elite offers a faint hope of better treatment by the new elite.

History reveals that advanced societies require a managerial class, and this managerial elite can take many forms: secular, religious, commercial, etc. As Turchin observed, complex societies in integrative phases generate expansive managerial elites, and the pool of aspirants who want to join the elite class grows proportionately.

But in the disintegrative phase, an economy's ability to support an ever-expanding elite class decays, and so the society produces more elite aspirants than available elite positions. Those expecting to join the elite class who are left behind create a rising pool of disgruntled, marginalized outsiders who feel entitled to managerial positions.

This class of disenfranchised elites destabilizes the status quo, as *expectations* and *relative status* are the foundations of human action, not measures of absolute wealth. We measure the wealth and status of others to assess how well we're doing, not the physical attributes of our well-being—quantity of food available to us, shelter, etc. As a result, the decline of social mobility is a more potent force than economic measures of income inequality suggest.

As the economy decays under the pressure of rising prices and stagnating wages, state revenues decline. In response to the incessant demands of elites and insiders, the state either borrows money to maintain its spending, or it devalues its currency to maintain the appearance of making the promised payments in full. As the state devalues its currency, the purchasing power of the currency drops, a reduction we call inflation: the identical good now costs more because the purchasing power of each unit of currency has declined.

We can add a fourth dynamic to Turchin's forces of disintegrative declines (stagnating wages, decaying state finances and the marginalization of entitled elites): the loss of shared purpose and the decline of social mobility.

The Corrupting Influence of Affluence

Previously we considered the economic and social dynamics that appear stable but which are non-linear due to hyper-coherence and the inherent fragility of social constructs. There is a third source of non-linearity, what we might call the *dynamics of decadence*. As affluence becomes the norm that is widely assumed to be permanent, shared purpose and sacrifice for the common good is replaced by self-absorbed decadence and an ethos of maximizing personal gain.

In his seminal essay *The Fate of Empires*, Sir John Glubb listed these core dynamics of imperial decline:

- a) A growing love of money as an end in itself
- b) A lengthy period of wealth and ease, which makes people complacent. They lose their edge; they forget the traits (confidence, energy, hard work) that built their civilization
- c) Selfishness and self-absorption
- d) Loss of any sense of duty to the common good

Glubb included the following in his list of the characteristics of decadence:

- An increase in frivolity, hedonism, materialism and the worship of unproductive celebrity
- A loss of social cohesion
- The willingness of an increasing number of people to live at the expense of a bloated bureaucratic state

Glubb's list may at first glance be largely psychological—self-aggrandizement and a focus on hedonistic pursuits—but the dynamics of decadence also have economic, political and social ramifications.

First and foremost, the aristocratic financial and political elites secured their position at the expense of social mobility by erecting barriers that protect them from competition from the lower ranks. In effect, they eliminated the risk posed by change by rigging the system to their benefit.

To fund their extravagant lifestyles, they took more of the earnings of those below them, widening the inequality between the aristocracy and commoners to extremes. Turchin reports that where the patricians of the Roman Republic had 10 or 20 times the wealth of an average Roman citizen, by the late stages of that Empire the elites possessed up to 200,000 times the wealth of the average commoner. The heavier burdens on the productive class and the decay of social mobility divested commoners of a financial stake in the system, and the concentration of political power in an oligarchy disenfranchised them of political influence.

When social mobility and shared purpose are lost, there is little motivation to contribute to a system that benefits the few at the expense of the many. People respond by reducing their productive participation and becoming dependents of the state, a phase captured by the phrase *Bread and Circuses* in the late Roman era, when a significant percentage of Rome's populace received free bread and access to costly entertainments in exchange for their political compliance.

Disenfranchised commoners with few prospects for advancement form a volatile political class. A small event can trigger a non-linear explosion that threatens the stability of a status quo that benefits the few at the expense of the many. To counter this threat, in Rome the elites bought the compliance and complicity of the masses with the aforementioned *Bread and Circuses*. Thus, as Glubb noted, the willingness to live off the state is a reflection of general decadence; if there is no other hedonistic pursuit within financial reach, then Bread and Circuses will do.

As the eventual collapse of decadent empires attests, Bread and Circuses are no long term substitute for social mobility, low barriers to accumulating capital and a political stake in the system. In the present era of decadence, Universal Basic Income (UBI) is the modern equivalent of Bread and Circuses. But buying off the disenfranchised doesn't transform an unstable system into a stable system; it merely masks the instability and postpones the inevitable collapse for a short while.

The core belief of decadent eras is that the status quo is so powerful and permanent that it can withstand the predations of the few and the Bread and Circuses lavished on the many. This is of course a false confidence. Every status quo is a social construct that is inherently non-linear. The decline of productive sectors, the divesture of commoners from ownership of productive assets, and the political disenfranchisement of commoners hollow out the economy and the society.

The Failure to Embrace Adaptation and New Ideas

The two other key characteristics of a state in terminal decline are complacency and intellectual sclerosis, which includes both a resistance to new ideas and new knowledge and what I term *a failure of imagination*—a profound inability to project the transition of the status quo from linear stability to non-linear instability as well as grasp the need for new ways of thinking as the only pathway with any hope of success.

Michael Grant described these causes of decline in his excellent account *The Fall of the Roman Empire*:

"There was no room at all, in these ways of thinking, for the novel, apocalyptic situation which had now arisen, a situation which needed solutions as radical as itself. (The Status Quo) attitude is a complacent acceptance of things as they are, without a single new idea.

This acceptance was accompanied by greatly excessive optimism about the present and future. Even when the end was only sixty years away, and the Empire was already crumbling fast, Rutilius continued to address the spirit of Rome with the same supreme assurance.

This blind adherence to the ideas of the past ranks high among the principal causes of the downfall of Rome. If you were sufficiently lulled by these traditional fictions, there was no call to take any practical first-aid measures at all."

These two failings—a complacent reliance on past grandeur and the rejection of new ideas—characterize the Chinese Imperial court in the Ming Dynasty (1368 to 1644 A.D.) and the subsequent Qing Dynasty (1644 to 1912 A.D.).

If we had to summarize the source of this complacent reliance on past glories and stubborn intellectual sclerosis, we can say it results from *a resistance to change rather than the embrace of change*, as any change threatens the elites' control of the status quo. Change is the mortal enemy of entrenched elites who understand that *change is unpredictable and thus a grave risk*. From the perspective of an entrenched technocratic elite, the lower risk strategy is to cling to the established ways, come what may.

Thus the Chinese court's response to the advances of the western powers was to cling even more tenaciously to the quasi-religious belief that changing anything established in the past would lead to disaster, as the very structure of Heaven and Earth rested on the old order being followed in every detail.

Ironically, this resistance to change sealed the empire's fate, since disaster is the only possible result of refusing to adapt and evolve to changing circumstances.

This is the ontological failing of all entrenched elites: adaptation will always be riskier than clinging to the past (i.e. *doing more of what's failed*), and so the institutional muscles and nervous systems required for successful adaption atrophy to the point that the elites' reluctant willingness to adapt as collapse looms is too little, too late.

The Diminishing Returns of Complexity

A number of authors have explored the role of increasing complexity in the demise of advanced civilizations, including Joseph Tainter and Thomas Homer-Dixon. As complexity increases, costs increase while the benefits of adding more complexity diminish.

Increasing complexity without commensurate increases in selective advantages pushes systems closer to the boundary between linear stability and non-linear instability.

The astonishing rise in the complexity of our everyday life is self-evident, as are the resulting increases in time, effort and money required to navigate this complexity. Increasingly, systems no longer function as planned, and sorting out the problems is a major project. This is not just the result of hyper-coherent complexity outgrowing our ability to manage interconnected layers of complexity; it is also the result of institutions protecting their employees and masking the organization's ineffectiveness by generating bureaucratic thickets (or moats if you prefer that analogy) that hamper transparency and accountability.

Ironically, the drive to reduce costs and increase efficiency serve to increase the fragility of complex systems, as redundancy is stripped out as an unneeded expense, buffers are thinned by just-in-time deliveries, staffing is cut to the minimum, and senior workers are retired to lower costs.

The ubiquity of advanced software might be expected to simplify complex processes, but this is not the case. For example, simple building permits that once took a day to process now take months. Examples abound in every aspect of everyday life: thousands of pages of new regulations issued by self-serving bureaucracies generate millions of lines of software code and require millions of hours of labor with very little real-world payoff. The lines at the Department of Motor Vehicles get longer, not shorter.

Complexity predates computers. The disintegrative stage of empires feature flurries of orders and regulations that no longer have any effect: the garrison staff has deserted or been wiped out; the tax officials are keeping whatever meager take they can skim from an impoverished populace, and the legions exist only in name.

At some point, the gains reaped by abandoning complexity far outweigh the benefits of shouldering the ever-heavier burdens of complexity.

The pointlessness of this accelerating rise in complexity has spawned the term *BS work*, which author David Graeber describes as work that everyone knows is meaningless: if it was no longer performed, no one would miss it, especially the people tasked with grinding it out.

Managing complexity is the lifeblood of bureaucracies and institutions, and so reducing complexity is anathema, a threat to the *raison d'etre* of the organization and to the security of its employees. There is no institutional pathway to reducing the complexity of the building code, for example; that would be considered counterproductive or even dangerous.

And so the only pathway available to reduce complexity is collapse: nobody will be left to enforce building codes on makeshift shanties.

Linear Systems and Thinking in a Non-Linear World

Let's summarize the response of a system optimized to linear thinking that's suddenly faced with non-linear dynamics: the traditional solution is to harden the system to protect the existing power structure. Like the Ming and Qing Dynasties, our status quo considers adaptation unnecessary. Like the Roman elites before the collapse of the Western Empire, our elites look to the past to comfort themselves that the status quo has what it takes to weather any crisis.

There's no need to become flexible or disrupt entrenched elites—just borrow more money. That's what America's power structure optimizes as the first and only response to any problem.

Need another trillion to finance absurdly expensive weaponry? Borrow it. Need another trillion to finance stock buybacks? Borrow it. Need another trillion to finance dividends? Borrow it. Need another trillion to fund an ineffective, bloated system of higher education? Borrow it. Need another trillion to fund tax breaks? Borrow it. Need another trillion to fund obscenely overpriced healthcare? Borrow it. And so on.

This is how the nation's public and private debt has ballooned to $70 trillion, dwarfing the nation's modest expansion of real-world goods and services. It now takes multiple dollars of additional debt to generate a few pennies of real-world growth.

We now depend on speculative bubbles to create a smoke-and-mirrors perception of wealth, not actual wealth earned via increasing productivity.

Borrowing money and inflating speculative bubbles is the easy path because these solutions enrich entrenched elites. Since they leave the power structure untouched, they meet no resistance, as speculative bubbles make everyone in the power structure wealthier.

America's centralized power structure optimizes linear projections of current stability to support complacent predictions of future stability. The nation's elites grossly overestimate the stability of the status quo and grossly underestimate the non-linearity of the nation's financial and social systems.

The cost of these make-believe solutions appear modest and the gains outsized, as the erosion of systemic resilience is hidden from view. Just as few in the power structure foresaw the non-linear consequences of the collapse of subprime lending in 2008, few grasp the non-linear consequences of exponentially rising debt and wealth/income inequality. Those who do are stymied by the system's resistance to structural change.

The power structure's response to the one non-linear crisis of this era, the Global Financial Meltdown of 2008-09, is telling: monumental efforts were made to avoid any change in that power structure. The nation's central bank and Treasury bailed out the financial sector with tens of trillions of dollars in subsidies, backstops and loan guarantees, protecting the system from any adaptation that could have disrupted the entrenched elites.

The managerial elites then engineered a decade of stimulus to expand public and private debt and inflate an unprecedented hyper-coherent speculative bubble in virtually all assets classes. In other words, the power structure pulled out all the stops to create an illusion of prosperity.

That the speculative wealth created was completely lopsided in favor of the top 5% (and within that elite, in favor of the top 1%) was not viewed as a flaw; the system is optimized to produce such asymmetric gains.

The immense damage done to the nation's buffers against future crises by these solutions is safely hidden from view. That is the nature of non-linear systems: thinning buffers issue few warning signs that collapse is imminent.

The managerial elites fail to see the causal connection between their solution to the crisis and soaring wealth/income inequality, a dynamic that is pushing the social order into non-linear instability. When the social order destabilizes, increasing credit and speculative bubbles won't save the system. In other words, the power structure's solution didn't actually stabilize the system; all it managed to do was widen the crisis from the financial sector to the social and political orders.

America's power structure is unprepared to navigate non-linear disruptions in finance, energy, resources and the social order. The managing elites don't understand the non-linearity of these structures and the potential for cascading collapses triggered by minor perturbations. What the managerial elites (think they) learned from the 2008-09 crisis is *we can borrow and manipulate our way out of any non-linear crisis*. This explains their tone deafness to the brewing social non-linearity of soaring wealth inequality and political oligarchy.

Lip service is paid to innovation, of course. But the sort of innovation that's welcomed is the linear kind that lowers costs and increases profits while leaving the power structure unchanged. But innovation can be non-linear as well, and brittle, centralized hierarchies are highly vulnerable to faster, better, cheaper alternatives that catch fire in the decentralized, fast-evolving informal economy the centralized hierarchies can't control.

If we set out to design a system devoid of flexibility, variation and resilience, a system incapable of navigating non-linear dynamics, a system designed to fail, we'd end up with a self-serving neofeudal oligarchy optimized to benefit the super-wealthy few and their entrenched technocrat managers at the expense of the many—in other words, the system we have right now.

SECTION II. The Rise of Neofeudalism and Oligarchy

Social constructs--the economy, government and society--have a formal structure of rules, laws and authority, and an informal structure of cultural norms that guide how things work in practicality.

Entrenched elites will tightly control any modifications of formal structure to ensure their control and ownership of wealth remains unthreatened. As a result, meaningful formal change only occurs when systemic crises leave the status quo leadership no other choice.

Thus adaptation tends to occur first in informal structures. For example, when a state's formal currency structure breaks down during hyper-inflation, the entrenched elites seek to limit alternative currencies as threats to their control. Informally, people turn to barter, black markets and cryptocurrencies to survive, all of which may be formally illegal.

In this way, informal structures act as flexible safety valves for the failure of formal structures to adapt to systemic failure or disruptive circumstances. This is one key dynamic in corruption: in dysfunctional formal systems, the only way to get anything done is to bribe officials who know how to get the necessary formal approvals.

The greater the dysfunction of the formal structure, the more reliant the economy will be on the informal structures of the black market and corruption.

This divergence between formal (legally sanctioned) and informal (unsanctioned) structures reflects the enormous gap between the entrenched classes holding virtually all the formal power and who also hold the vast majority of the formal wealth (i.e. legal ownership of land, stocks, bonds, enterprises, concessions, etc.) vs. the marginalized, disenfranchised commoners who only have access to highly contingent informal wealth (squatters rights, a stretch of sidewalk for selling wares, etc.) and little effective political voice.

In highly dysfunctional economies, entrenched elites tolerate the informal structures because these are less impactful on their wealth than formalized welfare ("Bread and Circuses"). The barrier between formal and informal systems is virtually impenetrable, a reality explored by Hernando De Soto in his book *The Mystery of Capital: Why Capitalism Triumphs in the West and Fails Everywhere Else*: formal structures of ownership are thickets of bureaucratic complexity that only the wealthy can afford to navigate.

Both the commoners and the entrenched elites understand the precarious nature of this asymmetric system: should entrenched elites tighten the screws on the informal economy too much, they risk sparking an open rebellion of the disenfranchised. Should commoners threaten the entrenched elites, it's entirely legal (in a system of law that exists to enforce the power of entrenched elites) to shut off the informal (and thus illegal) water taps and electrical connections that the commoners depend on and bulldoze the shantytowns that are their only shelter.

Less dysfunctional societies keep a tight rein on informal alternatives, forcing everyone but the most marginalized into the formal structure of employment or welfare. The recent dramatic rise of abject homelessness in U.S. cities is an example of what happens when informal structures have been eradicated by strict enforcement of formal rules: there is literally nowhere to go but the streets and freeway overpasses. Camping on sidewalks and begging are illegal, of course, but America's prisons are already full to bursting, so the formal enforcement mechanisms are hamstrung by burgeoning homelessness.

In prior eras, cramped, often-decrepit low-cost housing was available to the marginalized and low-income in what were labeled "slums" and "ghettos". Redevelopment that greatly enriched developers and lenders eradicated this pool of low-cost housing in favor of luxury apartments, a handful of which are available at modest discounts to the marginalized who meet strict formal standards of disability and moderate income. These units are not low-cost; they are simply subsidized by the high rents paid by market-rate tenants. Personally, I was only able to work my way through university and obtain a bachelor's degree in four years because there were still pockets of low-cost, often-decrepit housing still available in the 1970s.

While formal structures are codified and enforced by institutionalized authority, much of their power rests not in legal statutes but in deeply ingrained cultural expectations and assumptions. Christopher Wickham's book, *The Inheritance of Rome: Illuminating the Dark Ages 400-1000 AD*, shows how the ingrained structure of the

Western Roman Empire continued to shape and inform the expectations of commoners and elites alike for hundreds of years after the demise of the formal structure of Roman power.

This legacy of loyalty to a central authority manifested 324 years after the collapse of the formal structures of the Western Roman Empire (circa 476 A.D.) in Charlemagne, who united much of Western Europe as the head of the Holy Roman Empire in 800 A.D. (Recall that the Eastern Roman Empire endured 1,000 years beyond its western counterpart, until the last remnants fell to the Ottomans in 1453 A.D.)

But beneath this top-level continuation of centralized authority, the complex web of patronage, commerce and centralized collection of taxes that bound the Roman world slowly unraveled. As central authority's ability to collect taxes and provide patronage faded, the legacy rights of commoners established by Rome were slowly chipped away by local authorities and transferred to the feudal nobility.

As Wickham explains, these rights included limited self-rule within village councils and ownership of land. These rights were extinguished by feudalism, which bound the peasantry to the nobilities' persons and estates. The resulting decentralization of power in a multitude of competing fiefdoms created obstacles to both the reassertion of centralized power of monarchy and commerce.

The formal structure of feudalism required payment in the form of the peasant's labor and a percentage of the peasants' agricultural output to the local aristocracy. Freedom of movement was prohibited, a form of indentured servitude that was only broken by the eventual rise of free commerce-centric cities which refused to recognize or enforce aristocratic control of those unlucky enough to be born on the nobles' estates.

In the current era, the old formal structures of feudalism have been replaced by new structures of control, divestiture and disenfranchisement that I term *neofeudalism*. The old formal rights of ownership and political participation have been abridged in practice by the concentrated power and wealth of entrenched elites—what I term *the New Nobility* or *New Aristocracy*--and the decay of commoners' social mobility and political influence.

In other words, the legal right to acquire productive capital and claim a political voice technically and legally remain, but in reality the levers of governance and financial power are in the hands of global corporations and the top 1% of households, and to a lesser degree in the top 10% managerial class that serves the interests of the New Nobility: technocrats, media editors/producers, professionals, lobbyists, etc.

Given that this new elite class effectively runs the formal machinery of the status quo, and has reaped on the order of 85% of the gains in wealth and income generated in the past decade, it's little wonder that the corporate media loudly proclaims that *the status quo is working wonderfully for me, so it must be working for everyone else, too.*

To fully understand neofeudalism, we must first differentiate between its two primary sources: 1) the initial conditions of an economy's ownership of capital and political power, and 2) the dynamics that slowly erode the original structure in favor of neofeudalism.

As an example of the first, consider the history of South American states, in which political independence was accompanied by the vast majority of the newly freed land being purchased by a handful of well-placed insiders. States in which the emperor, sultan, monarch, colonial satrapy or ruling clique effectively owned or controlled all land. They rarely divided the capital amongst commoners once the old order fell; the capital was transferred from the central authority to well-placed insiders.

Once the capital is in the grasp of a financial and political aristocracy, it's difficult to distribute the capital more broadly without a revolution, and even then, one set of self-serving rascals is typically replaced by another set of (initially idealistic) rascals.

The key point here is that *broad-based ownership of productive capital* (i.e. capital that generates permanent income streams) is the necessary foundation for political power to be similarly broadly distributed. Without widely distributed ownership of productive capital, neofeudal oligarchy is the result, where a powerful aristocracy bribes voters (as in India) or pulls the levers of power behind the façade of elections.

Given that asymmetry of ownership and power were present from the beginning, everyone implicitly understands these societies are incapable of changing the power structure. Paid lackeys glorify the facades of democracy and free markets, but everyone knows these are facades.

For an example of the second source of neofeudalism, where dynamics slowly erode the original structure in favor of neofeudalism, we will focus on the U.S., though the same principles can be found throughout the developed world, which is, after all, now tightly interconnected (hyper-coherent) via globalization. The dynamics of this advanced form of neofeudalism are primarily financial: financialization and neoliberal globalization which have generated enormous premiums for mobile capital, monopolies and specialized expertise in software and finance, while devaluing labor's value in fields that can be profitably offshored or mechanized with software and robotics.

The primary dynamic here is the gradual erosion of widely distributed, independent ownership of productive capital—the necessary foundation for democracy that is truly representative and not merely a convenient façade for aristocratic rule—in favor of highly concentrated ownership of capital and political power.

The secondary dynamic is the ability to use the immense wealth concentrated by financialization and neoliberal globalization to purchase political power, which creates an oligarchy. This is how neofeudal concentration of income and wealth translates into political power in America's pay-to-play form of advocacy government: those with wealth buy access and influence, and those without wealth have little say. A recent study, *Testing Theories of American Politics: Elites, Interest Groups, and Average Citizens*, found that voters have very little power in the U.S., effectively making the US an oligarchy.

The formal façade of elected representatives provides excellent cover for the New Aristocracy, another reality we can see in both developed and developing economies.

The dominance of state-controlled markets is the foundation of neofeudal oligarchy: control the state, and you can protect state-enforced cartels and monopolies. Control the market and you can buy political power with the profits. (We'll cover the neofeudal state-market structure shortly.)

This divergence of formal rights and the actual structure of wealth and power is the core characteristic of neofeudalism and oligarchy. American citizens retain the right to cast a vote, but their vote has little actual influence over the government's decisions. Every citizen retains the legal right to acquire productive capital, but only the top 5% own meaningful amounts of productive capital, and the majority of this capital is owned by the New Nobility, the top 0.1% of American households.

The gradual erosion of commoners' political and economic power and the rise of a neofeudal aristocracy leaves our cultural expectations intact. Thus students earning university degrees expect to find secure employment, newly elected representatives expect to make real changes, those going to work for progressive organizations expect to solve pressing social problems, and so on—yet none of this is possible in the current power structure.

All these cultural expectations remain enshrined in formal systems—one citizen, one vote, acceptance on merit rather than privilege, freedom of movement, representational governance, and so on—but they no longer have the power to correct the structural sources of decay.

Instead, students find their diplomas have little market value except for the few who graduate from select universities in select fields. Newly elected representatives find that any independence is punished by the party machinery. Idealists find they cannot change the systemic roots of the problems. Everywhere, people are co-opted or corrupted by perverse incentives, sclerotic bureaucracies, self-serving insiders, crushing debt loads and all the other realities of a highly asymmetric neofeudal oligarchy.

The tremendous divergence between the experiential reality of America's neofeudal power structure and the idealized expectations of its people is the wellspring of non-linear social unrest. No amount of cajoling by the managerial class (the top 10%) can change this, and the shrill insistence of the managerial class that *all is well because we're doing well* only further discredits the claim that all is well.

This divergence feeds an explosive sense of collective injustice: the insiders have hardened the system to their benefit at the expense of everyone else. In cultures where commoners have low expectations— "the aristocracy exploits us but that's the way of the world"—there is little divergence of experience and expectations. But in cultures that inculcate their populace with lofty expectations—anyone can be president, do what you love and the money will follow, there are no limits on what you can achieve, etc.--this profound divergence of expectations and the real world fuels a highly combustible reservoir of injustice that needs only a spark to burst into non-linear crisis.

Just as the mandarins of the Ming and Qing Dynasties and the elites of Rome were offended by suggestions that the old order was failing, most of America's managerial elite are offended by the characterization of the United States as a neofeudal oligarchy. They view themselves as living proof that meritocracy, autonomy and rule of law are the operative principles of American life.

But these principles don't change the power structure of the U.S. any more than the meritocracy of China's civil service changed the power structure of the Qing society, or the autonomy afforded Roman citizens changed the power structure of the late Roman era, an era in which the aristocracy gained immense wealth and political power at the expense of the commoners.

Anyone seriously interested in a successful national strategy (as opposed to a politically correct façade) must accept the functional realities of America's power structure. They must also understand that highly centralized wealth and power are intrinsically destabilizing, and that centralized hierarchical institutions are in effect designed to fail catastrophically during non-linear crises.

The few who own the majority of America's productive wealth and power are anticipating that they will be able to exit any crisis with their current wealth and power in hand. This is of course what the Roman and Qing aristocracies believed as well, right up until the entire status quo collapsed.

Those tasked with designing a successful national strategy for the U.S. must first be willing to jettison the neofeudal economic order and its political oligarchy in favor of resilient structures designed to serve the common good.

The Structure of Neofeudalism

I have covered financialization, neoliberalism and globalization at length in my previous books, and for brevity's sake I will limit this discussion to sketching how combining these three systems results in a neofeudal oligarchy.

There are various definitions of financialization, but the core dynamic is simple: low-cost, essentially unlimited credit is extended by central banks to those at the very apex of the financial system—financiers, banks and corporations. Armed with this credit, these entities buy up the productive assets of the economy. They can outbid less well-connected bidders because everyone below them has to pay a higher rate of interest. They can then lend this low-cost credit to everyone below them at higher rates of interest, reaping profits from capital they borrow rather than earn or save.

Anyone able to borrow $1 billion dollars at 1% annual interest can do very well for themselves buying Treasury or low-risk corporate bonds yielding 3%. Unfortunately only those at the apex of the system have access to unlimited low-cost central bank credit. This restricted access generates vast inequalities of wealth and income by its very design.

In other words, financialization is the result of a spectacular expansion of credit and leverage at the top of the wealth-power pyramid. Those few at the top then have the means to commodify financial instruments collaterized by previously low-risk assets such as housing. The resulting explosion of speculative gains rewards the few (those with access to central bank credit) at the expense of the many (borrowers, i.e. *debt-serfs* in a neofeudal economy that is dependent on ever-expanding borrowing).

Another way to describe the same dynamic is: *financialization is the result of leverage and information asymmetry replacing productive investment as the source of wealth creation*. That is, when financial insiders profit from knowledge that outsiders cannot obtain, and leveraging credit is more profitable that investing in innovation, the economy has been financialized. When speculating with credit is more profitable than innovating new goods and services, the real economy is hollowed out while wealth and income flow to those at the top of the financialization game.

As their real (adjusted for inflation) income stagnates, commoners fill the gap between lagging income and rising prices by borrowing more money. This liability (debt) is a highly profitable income stream for the elites who own the debt (student loans, mortgages, auto loans, etc.)

As for the wealth of the commoners, if we examine the supposed wealth of the middle class/working class (however you define these classes, the defining characteristic of both is a reliance on labor for income, as opposed to income earned by capital), we find the primary capital asset is the family home, which, as I have explained elsewhere, is in essence, a form of consumption rather than a source of income.

This housing wealth is far from secure; rather, it is contingent on the speculative bubble in housing not bursting. Since speculative bubbles always eventually burst, this housing "wealth" is temporary, a reality revealed in the bursting of the previous housing bubble in 2006-08.

Given that most households owe a mortgage on their home, owners' equity is an artifact of the current speculative bubble, a temporary mirage. It is not the equivalent of traditional savings.

The same can be said for stock and bond holdings, which are typically held in retirement and pension accounts: the current gains are a temporary artifact of unprecedented speculative bubbles.

Ultimately, all pensions, both public and private, are controlled by central authorities, even though formal ownership is nominally held by commoners. Just ask middle-class Venezuelans what their pensions are worth now that central authorities have debased their national currency.

As for the rest of commoners' wealth: the value of used vehicles, furniture and other possessions is pennies on the dollar.

Once the speculative bubbles burst, only the relatively few commoners who have profitable family enterprises or income-producing assets that are debt-free will own any productive wealth. The majority of commoners will be left with very little wealth and an abundance of unpayable debts. Setting aside niceties, their status as debt-serfs will be revealed for all to see. This will be a highly combustible realization for those who reckoned their middle class status was secure.

Neoliberalism is the ideological belief that the social order is defined by markets: if markets are free, then participants, society and the political order will also free. While there is historical evidence to support this principle—free markets tend to go hand in hand with religious, intellectual and political freedom--the reality is that markets are anything but free.

Such a conceptual framework is the perfect enabler for the dominance of leveraged capital, i.e. financialized neofeudalism. In this "free market," those with access to nearly-free credit can outbid everyone who must rely on savings from earned income to buy assets. In a "free market" where those with access to unlimited credit are *more equal than everyone else*, the ability of wage earners to acquire income-producing assets is intrinsically limited by the financial system that makes credit scarce for the many and abundant for the few.

Much has been written about globalization. For the purposes of this discussion, the basics are enough: globalization boils down to the *commoditization of everything*: capital, financial instruments, currencies, goods and services, and labor, i.e. *labor arbitrage*, as workers must compete with labor around the world. (When a product is interchangeable with one produced elsewhere, we say it's a commodity. In our globalized economy, credit, labor, software and services are all commoditized; it no longer matters where the credit is issued, the work is performed, or the product is manufactured.)

A globalized, financialized economy places an enormous premium on *mobile capital*, capital that can be shifted by a keystroke to avoid devaluation or earn a higher return. Thus the factory that opened to much hoopla last year may suddenly be closed this year if higher returns can be found elsewhere.

As a result, mobile capital now influences much more than just the financial sector. As former Federal Reserve Chairman Alan Greenspan noted in 2008: *"Thanks to globalization, policy decisions in the US have been largely replaced by global market forces. National security aside, it hardly makes any difference who will be the next President."*

Turning from mobile capital to the assets of commoners, housing and pensions: these are *stranded capital*, forms of capital that are not mobile unless they are liquidated well before crises or expropriations occur. This places the burdens of navigating global crises that could upend the domestic economy on commoners. Such offloading of risk to those without the training or experience to manage such risk is one of the most damaging consequences of neoliberal neofeudalism.

Up to this point, we've been discussing the financial power structure of neofeudalism. But this is only half the picture; we must now consider the cost structure of neofeudalism, and examine why prices are rising at rates far above the officially stated inflation rate.

To understand the extortionist nature of feudal power structures, let's return to the late Middle Ages, at the height of feudalism, and imagine we're trying to get a boatload of goods to the nearest city to sell. As we drift down the river, we're constantly being stopped and charged a toll for transiting one small fiefdom after another. When we finally reach the city, there's an entry fee for bringing our goods to market. Note that none of these fees were payments for improvements to transport or for services rendered; they were simply extortion. This was the economic structure of feudalism: petty fiefdoms levied extortionate fees that funded the lifestyles of the nobility.

This is similar to today in our modern neofeudal economy, where we pay ever higher fees for services that are degrading, not improving. This is the essence of extortion: we don't get any improvement in goods and services for the extra money we're forced to pay.

Consider higher education: costs are soaring while the value of the "product"--a college diploma--declines. What extra value are students receiving for the doubling of tuition and fees? The short answer is none. College diplomas are in over-supply, and studies such as *Academically Adrift* have found that a majority of students learn remarkably little of value in college.

As I explain in my book *The Nearly Free University and the Emerging Economy*, the solution is to *accredit the student, not the institution*. What should be measured and rewarded is how much the student actually learned, not whether they met the institution's academic requirements.

Consider healthcare: has the quality of healthcare tripled along with costs? Are Americans significantly healthier as the per capita costs of healthcare have tripled? The aggregate health of Americans has arguably declined, while the stresses placed on frontline care providers by the ever-heavier burdens of compliance have increased.

What about the $200 hammers and $300 million F-35 aircraft of the defense industry? Once again, as costs have soared, the quality and effectiveness of the products being supplied have arguably declined.

How about state and local government services? Are they improving as taxes and junk fees rise? Once again, government services are often declining in quality as taxes and fees continue to increase by leaps and bounds. In sector after sector, the quality of the goods and services has declined while costs have soared. This is the acme of neofeudalism: insiders and the New Nobility are skimming fortunes as prices skyrocket and the quality of the goods and services provided plummet.

This is nothing but extortion. The cartels and state agencies raise prices and we're forced to pay them, just as feudal commoners were forced to pay.

The key to understanding how neofeudal extortion has become the dominant source of earnings and profits is the symbiotic relationship between the market and the state: the state manages the markets to maintain cartels and quasi-monopolies, as this can enrich those buying political influence and guarantee the state reliable profits to tax.

The only possible result of combining financialization, neoliberalism and globalization is a neofeudal system that benefits the few at the expense of the many; a system of asymmetric wealth and power that is intrinsically destabilizing and thus prone to non-linear disruption.

Once again, note that the insiders (the top 10% managerial class) will emphatically reject the reality of such an extortionist power structure because they are benefiting from that structure. It is asking a great deal of anyone to accept that the system that issues their pay is extortionist, exploitive and vulnerable to collapse. Yet anyone who sincerely wants the U.S. to survive the inevitable demise of an extortionist neofeudal power structure will have to set aside their own stake in the system and focus on resilient, flexible structures completely unlike those that currently dominate the economy and society.

The Limits of the Market and the State

I have covered the topic in previous books, but it's necessary to mention, however briefly, that the idea that the market and/or the state can fix what's broken runs into the intrinsic limits of both structures.

As I explained in my book *Resistance, Revolution, Liberation*, the state's *ontological imperative* is to ceaselessly expand its control and budget, lest anything left outside its control become a threat. In integrative stages, this expansion appears beneficial, potentially yielding some version of the much-admired Scandinavian model of the state managing a vibrant private sector to provide generous universal welfare benefits to all.

The present-day story of the state's expanding power in disintegrative stages has yet to be written, but history has not been kind to states that continue to expand complexity, regulation and enforcement in disintegrative eras, especially expansions funded by borrowing money on a vast scale.

As for the much-vaunted market, it is intrinsically incapable of differentiating between much different things, as I explain in my book *Money and Work Unchained*. In the logic of the market, the last schools of wild tuna fetch a nice price for being scarce, while farmed fish offer a ready substitute. But wild fisheries, being complex ecosystems, are different from fish farms. The market equates the two because it's incapable of valuing ecosystems and externalities such as biodiversity. Markets price scarcity and demand in the present moment, and so they are ontologically incapable of valuing everything that cannot be reduced to a price discovered by supply and demand.

This includes social cohesion, shared purpose, meaningful work, and a great many other essential components of the social construct we call the economy—a social construct that cannot be reduced to a market, despite the best efforts of ideologues to do so.

Those who believe the core problem is lack of *aggregate demand* for more goods and services believe the solution is simple and obvious: the state should distribute Universal Basic Income (UBI) to everyone, funded by higher taxes on the wealthy. This would give everyone the money needed to buy more goods and services, i.e. expand *aggregate demand,* thus driving growth which drives prosperity. (Never mind that infinite growth on a finite planet poses a fundamental obstacle.)

Those who believe the problem is that markets have been hobbled by the state also believe the solution is simple and obvious: free markets will solve all problems by discovering the price of everything, and thus incentivize everyone to develop substitutes for whatever is scarce (farmed fish substituted for wild fisheries, solar panels for oil, etc.). The belief is that unfettered markets will drive growth which drives prosperity.

Now imagine these being presented as the solutions to what ailed the Western Roman Empire circa 456 A.D., 20 years before the final implosion of the empire, or in Qing Dynasty China in 1892, 20 years prior to the final collapse of the dynasty. What ailed these tottering systems was not a lack of aggregate demand or hobbled markets; these systems were structurally brittle and fragile, completely lacking the flexibility and adaptability needed to navigate non-linear upheaval.

These illusory, magical-thinking solutions—Universal Basic Income and unfettered markets--are only embraced because they don't require any changes in the power structure.

The Mindset of the Elite: Denial, Complacency, Appeals to the Past, Faith in Technology

The technocrat managerial, financial and political elites of the U.S. are currently following the same path previously taken by the ancient

Roman and Chinese elites: denial that the status quo is not just dysfunctional but indeed incapable of navigating non-linear crises; denial that the system benefits the few at the expense of the many; a complacent, hubris-soaked confidence in their managerial expertise and in the permanence of the status quo; appealing to the past as evidence that all challenges will be surmounted without changing the power structure; and protecting the privileges of the entrenched elite rather than risk adaptation.

As for new ideas, there are none. From the perspective of America's managerial elite, there is no need for new ideas: the faith that technocratic expertise and technological innovations will save us is enough. The profit potential of the market and the wise guidance of the state bureaucracy will ensure that whatever becomes scarce and costly will be replaced by something that is cheap and abundant.

This arrow of history will never fall to earth, as they believe recent history shows: once oil becomes costly, then fracking makes it affordable again. If healthcare becomes unaffordable, new technologies will arise to heal us all with cheap new treatments. If soil becomes depleted, we'll grow food in hydroponic towers. The belief is that there is literally no problem that can't be solved by new technology that will enrich its investors and developers and benefit all humankind as it disperses through the global economy.

Granted, there are certainly many examples of this: antibiotics, the Internet and mobile telephony, to name a few. And certainly if technology solves all problems, then there's no need for flexible, resilient, adaptable social constructs. Universal Basic Income (UBI) would take care of everyone left behind and boost aggregate demand, and markets would reward everyone developing new technologies. The neofeudal system dominated by an elite would remain untouched. This has become the mantra, embraced as the new religion of the elites.

But unlike previous religions, it is taken as scientific fact. While it is certainly comforting to reduce social constructs and a world of interconnected ecosystems and limited resources to problems that will all be magically fixed by managerial expertise and new technology, is it as grounded in reality as the faithful believe?

Debt Serfdom

As noted in the previous section, our economy is based on mass consumption funded by credit (finance) and rising wages (labor), enabled by cheap abundant energy and low inflation. Our social and political system is based on the broad-based distribution of capital (ownership of enterprises and property) which translates into a political stake.

As a generality, ownership of small businesses and property is characteristic of the middle class, which is the foundation of mass consumption and democracy.

How did an economy and society based on a large, stable middle class devolve to a neofeudal structure of an insecure, hollowed-out, politically impotent middle class dominated by an oligarchy?

There are several dynamics behind this systemic divesture of capital and power.

Let's start by noting that *labor* includes all paid work: wages, salaries, bonuses, etc. While many kinds of human labor are unpaid, for this discussion we're defining labor as *work that earns an income*. This covers the range from hedge fund managers earning $10 million a year for their work to people earning minimum wage in a part-time job.

Capital includes the traditional forms of capital such as cash, land, factories, tools, stocks and bonds—*tangible capital*—and *intangible forms of capital* that have become increasingly important in our knowledge-based economy: human capital (skills and knowledge), social capital (being able to work well with others and maintain a network of collaboration) and cultural capital (values and social norms).

Tangible capital typically generates a *passive income*—interest, dividends or capital gains—that results not from work but from *ownership of the capital*. Capital that accrues passive income is typically *tradable*, meaning that it can be bought and sold in the marketplace. Examples include commercial property, stocks and bonds.

If we look at the economy as a whole, we intuitively understand that if labor's share of total income declines, wage earners will have less opportunity to save the money needed to buy capital. If more of the economy's total income flows to passively owned capital, that gives the already-wealthy owners of capital the means to buy more capital. We can summarize this as *the rich get richer*.

Labor's share of the economy has been stagnating for decades. This has forced financial authorities to make credit widely available, so that households can fill the widening gap between rising expenses and stagnating income with debt. Debt transfers income from borrowers— those earning income from labor-- to the owners of the debt—those receiving the passive income of interest paid on the debt.

As the average household becomes increasingly dependent on debt to fund higher education, home ownership and living expenses, income increasingly flows from labor to capital—the owners of the debt who receive the interest paid by borrowers.

This expansion of credit benefits capital at the expense of labor in two ways: it funnels income from labor to capital (interest on the expanding debt), and it increases the dependency of wage-earners on credit, making labor beholden to capital.

As noted earlier, the financialization of housing has turned a stable asset in which home equity was once the equivalent of savings into a speculative asset prone to frenzied bubbles and busts. Only those with the aptitude, experience and luck to be successful traders can navigate speculative markets, and the average homeowner is ill-prepared to buy low, sell high, wait for a bottom, etc. How can anyone who buys at most a few properties in their entire lifetime master speculative trading? This conversion of stable assets into speculative assets puts the average middle-class worker at an extreme disadvantage to professional speculators and money managers.

As financialization has eroded the middle class's ability to acquire capital, globalization and the economy's dependence on rising corporate profits to justify soaring stock prices have eroded wage-earners' security and agency (control of one's livelihood and life). Workers have little control over their work environment because most labor has been commoditized. Workers are largely interchangeable, and corporate managers are pressed to reduce labor costs to increase profits and thus preserve their own job security.

Self-employment and small business were once mainstays of the middle class that offered agency and the means to acquire productive (income-producing) capital. Over-regulation, high overhead and rising costs have limited opportunities for self-employment to those with substantial expertise along with sufficient starting capital and appetite for risk.

According to IRS data, only 4 million taxpayers out of 150 million tax returns (2.6%) took the deduction for sole proprietors who pay their own healthcare insurance. This reflects the modest number of self-employed taxpayers whose income is high enough to afford to buy their own health insurance.

In aggregate, these dynamics have generated outsized rewards for those who already own capital, and reduced the opportunities to build capital for everyone else. The net result is *debt-serfdom*, a state of dependence on debt and corporate-state jobs that pay just enough for workers to be able to service their personal debts and consume enough to keep the mass-consumer society afloat, but not enough to acquire meaningful capital unless the worker is willing to make extraordinary efforts and take extraordinary risks.

According to recent (2016) IRS income data, only 6% of taxpayers reported capital gains, and most of those gains (63%) went to the top 0.16%, the 250,000 out of 150 million tax returns that reported earnings of $1 million or more.

These statistics reflect the tremendous asymmetry of capital gains: very few middle-class taxpayers own enough productive capital to generate either meaningful passive income or capital gains. Since labor's share of the economy continues sliding, the majority of households must borrow more to maintain their standard of living, since their earnings are declining when adjusted for inflation.

This is debt-serfdom. Politically, America's serfs have the right to move, but this freedom of movement amounts to moving allegiance from one corporate-state fiefdom to another; the bondage of debt and indentured dependence on labor remain.

For all the reasons outlined in this section, our current state of debt-serfdom and neofeudalism lack the stability of the enforced serfdom of the Middle Ages. Our debt serfdom is explosively non-linear, because as debt-serfs we no longer have a stake in the system or a reason to sacrifice to maintain it.

SECTION III. Energy, Credit, Consumption and Inflation

All forms of money and all promises of entitlements are nothing but claims on future extraction of energy: oil, electricity, etc. Without abundant, cheap energy, the global economy freezes. If there isn't enough energy available to power the global economy, there will be little for money to buy.

We can create money digitally, but we can't create oil or electricity with a few keystrokes.

So the master resource is energy—not just any form of energy, but transportable, high-density energy to fuel aircraft, trucks, trains and ships, manufacture materials, chemicals, medicines, fertilizers, etc., and power the billions of machines and devices that make up the global economy.

Will there be enough cheap, abundant energy in the future? There are two camps, and very little common ground between the two.

One camp holds that fossil fuels are being depleted far faster than most people realize and it will be impossible to replace this energy at current prices and at current levels of investment with other sources of energy.

The other camp holds that fossil fuels are still abundant and that new technologies will enable the extraction of this energy at reasonable cost. This camp also holds that nuclear technologies (fusion, new forms of fission), wind and solar can be readily ramped up to replace fossil fuels should the need arise.

Each camp has three sets of advocates: one that seeks evidence to support their faith, one that is paid to seek evidence to support their camp's position, and a much smaller one that actively seeks to collate data and research the facts of the matter: how much oil is actually extractable with current technologies, how much investment will be required to extract and process this oil, real-world progress in fusion reactors, the cost of scaling up wind and solar collectors, and so on.

We can dispense with the first two sets of advocates in both camps. This leaves us with relatively small groups who are being paid to assemble a fact-based understanding of energy without regard to the impact on vested interests.

It's not that difficult to separate the wheat from the chaff in energy. As a general rule, much of the optimism is based on extrapolations of technology that aren't even off the lab table, much less scalable to global production.

Even if the new technology moves from the lab to a working model, where will the money come from to scale it up to useful levels of production? As a general rule, all the proposed technologies remain expensive, despite claims that costs will inevitably descend to near-zero.

The key here is to set aside pie-in-the-sky forecasts and study the practicalities and costs. Consider paint that generates electricity. Wouldn't it be great to collect electricity on every external painted surface on the planet?

How much does it cost to manufacture this paint? How is the feeble current being generated collected? Where is it stored? Is this storage unit connected to the grid? How is the wattage boosted to usable levels? How much net energy is actually available after this conversion? What is the rate of decline in the electrical generation of the painted surface? Does the paint generate enough current to justify the considerable expense of the collection and storage systems? What is the replacement cycle for the paint, collection and storage systems? What are the lifecycle maintenance costs for these systems? How much of the electrical generation capacity is degraded by peeling, fading, etc.?

Once hard data is collected to answer all these questions, the potential of paint to generate meaningful, affordable quantities of electricity dims considerably. The same can be said of other technologies being touted by optimists: the full lifecycle costs—the sums needed to manufacture, install, maintain and replace (note that these systems don't last forever)—sodium reactors, photovoltaic roofing, wind farms, etc. are substantial and cannot be reduced to near-zero.

The best current estimates of total alternative energy production (not counting hydroelectric) globally is around 3% of total energy consumption. This is after years of global investment on the order of $250 billion annually.

If we're not being paid to turn a blind eye to facts, this is sobering. How much investment will it take to scale up alternative energy production to a third of global energy consumption? Given that the energy infrastructure—the grid, storage, smart systems, etc.—is itself a critical component of any large-scale alternative energy generation system, the cost will likely be on the same scale as the gross national product (GDP) of the world's largest economies.

If the world has invested several trillion dollars in the past decade and managed to replace a mere 3% of global energy production, this suggests that investing the equivalent of the U.S. GDP of $20 trillion would make a dent but still may not be enough to ramp up alternative energy production to a third of current consumption—the vast majority of which is fossil fuels: coal, natural gas and oil.

The other problem is energy is itself a non-linear system. The line between scarcity and sufficiency is thin; the loss of a few million barrels a day of oil quickly moves prices far more than the modest percentage decline in production.

Timelines in the energy sector are long. A revolution or war can cut oil production by millions of barrels a day in a matter of weeks, but it takes years to develop new oil and gas fields, which are increasingly located in extreme settings (arctic seabeds, etc.) or politically unstable nations. The same can be said of offshore wind farms, large solar arrays and all the other pieces of alternative energy.

Then there's the issue energy analyst Nate Hagens summarized as *renewables are more accurately replaceables*, meaning that a renewable-energy solar panel only lasts 20 years and will need to be replaced. (And this doesn't even address the reduction in energy produced if the panel isn't regularly cleaned, or the possibility that some of the array's components will fail to reach their presumed 20 year lifespan).

This increases the expense of any large-scale alternative energy system considerably, because we don't have the luxury of simply adding new capacity—we have to replace worn out components, too. The larger the installed base, the greater the cost of replacing worn-out components.

We also don't have the luxury of waiting for some new technology that might move from the lab to experimentation to production a decade or two hence. Global energy production is currently stable, but the quantity of new oil deposits being discovered is less than the oil currently being extracted: we're not discovering enough to replace what we're consuming.

Much has been written about the remarkable increase in U.S. fossil fuel production as a result of fracking technologies, which benefit from mobile rigs and relatively low costs when compared to $2 billion open ocean platforms. What receives less attention is the high depletion rates of the new wells and the financial losses incurred by the fracking industry ($5 billion in losses). Most new fracked wells yield the majority of their production within 18 to 24 months. After that, yields decline precipitously. Given the financial losses, the fracking industry is effectively being subsidized by the financial sector.

Despite the dramatic increase in domestic fossil fuel production, the U.S. currently still imports around 20% of its consumption of fossil fuels (3.7 million barrels of oil a day imported in 2017). In total energy, the U.S. imported 7.3 quadrillion British thermal units (quads) of energy. (Source: the U.S. Energy Information Administration—EIA.)

Meanwhile, the pool of global oil available for export is drying up as rising domestic demand within oil-exporting nations soaks up more of the oil production. As populations rise, so do demands for a share of the oil wealth and all the goods that consume oil in their manufacture. Since the oil wealth buys outside expertise, goods and services, there is little pressure to construct a diverse, productive economy (a.k.a. *the oil curse*). The net result is that global oil production could remain stable but the amount available for export to consuming nations could drop below the level needed to sustain the economies of the oil-consuming nations.

Putting this all together, the high depletion rates of fracking and the industry's insatiable need for cheap credit suggest that the current boom in U.S. production may enter diminishing returns much sooner than optimists expect.

Interestingly, the EIA has published a forecast that includes a range of scenarios, one of which is where the U.S. becomes a net exporter of fossil fuels in the 2030's if prices are high enough to justify the higher costs of extraction, processing and transport. Such a scenario, while sounding perhaps initially positive for the U.S., raises the issue of the future cost of energy, i.e. the affordability of energy for the average household, which is experiencing declining real (i.e. adjusted for inflation) income. As analysts Gail Tverberg and Richard Heinberg have explained, the economic growth the status quo requires to keep afloat is dependent on *affordable* energy, that is, energy which doesn't cost so much that the bottom 80% of the households with stagnant incomes can't afford to maintain their consumption of other products and services.

If energy costs spike higher, the result is recession, as consumer spending and the ability to service more debt both drop sharply. Given the non-linear nature of energy, it's only a matter of time before the supply falls far short of demand. Any such imbalance will yield non-linear disruptions; a modest 5% shortfall in oil can trigger price increases of 50% or more, an output/result that is an order of magnitude larger than the input/cause.

Apologists like to point to energy's diminishing role in America's GDP as evidence the cost of energy no longer matters much. But this is illusory: the cost of energy is embedded in everything, and shortages of liquid fuels quickly disrupt the economy, regardless of energy's relatively modest share of GDP.

We can now understand the non-linear nature of global energy and the multiple points of fragility. Current production is entirely dependent on cheap, abundant credit, which is itself non-linear. The investment needed to replace fossil fuels with renewables is in the tens of trillions of dollars, sums so large that the current system cannot fund all existing credit demands and the additional sums required to build out renewable energy on a global scale.

As the EIA implicitly states in its forecasts, the costs of extracting liquid fossil fuels must rise once the easy-to-get oil has been depleted and only hard-to-get, costly liquid fuels are left. This raises the affordability barrier: how can the bottom 80% afford higher energy and still maintain its profligate consumer borrowing and spending with stagnating incomes? The obvious answer is that they can't.

As many analysts have explained, the postwar global economy that expanded rapidly from 1950 on the abundance of affordable oil is an industrial economy that is highly dependent on the transportation complex—private vehicles, trucks, air travel, shipping—and other oil-dependent industries that are the mainstay of manufacturing and credit. Consider the global importance of manufacturing, maintaining and financing private vehicles. Affordable private transport enabled the vast expansion of suburbia and much of the built environment of the past 70 years.

As the price of energy rises hand-in-hand with the costs of extracting hard-to-get oil, the inflation-adjusted incomes of the bottom 80% decline and speculative bubbles in debt, housing and stock deflate, what happens to these households' ability to buy, maintain and fuel the one-car-per-person fleet that enables our currently built environment? The bottom 60% of American households have almost no savings and high debt loads; many can only afford leased vehicles with limited number of miles allowed per year, as they can't afford to buy and maintain even a used vehicle.

There is a fantasy that electric cars will replace the hundreds of millions of existing oil-fueled vehicles, but even a cursory glance at the lifecycle costs of electric vehicles and the enormous expansion of electricity required (recall the tens of trillions of dollars in investment required to build enough renewable capacity to make a difference) reveals this as magical thinking.

There is no escaping this trap: if the U.S. invests its income to service the enormous debt required to replace tens of millions of vehicles and build a new electrical grid and generation capacity, there won't be enough income left to maintain current levels of consumption. Once the rate of consumer debt expansion declines, consumption falls and the economy enters a recession that can't be fixed by inflating a new asset bubble, a solution that only enriches the top 10%.

It's also a fantasy to think that the top 10% buying new electric cars will stave off recession, or that their income/consumption will fund the enormous maintenance costs of the current auto-centric infrastructure.

A system that's unaffordable to the bottom 80% without vast subsidies cannot survive. The subsidies will all be borrowed, increasing a debt load that is already perilously high.

None of this is insider knowledge. It's all available from industry and mainstream-media sources.

The problem is the same one that sank the Qing Dynasty and the Western Roman Empire—appeals to the past and magical thinking (in this era, quasi-religious faith in technology) are easier than facing trade-offs that require sustained sacrifice. Entrenched elites will resist making sacrifices, and the bottom 90% will follow suit: why should the many sacrifice to maintain a power structure that enriches the few at their expense?

Why Inflation Is Inevitable

We can now tell the story of our economy and inflation.

Energy defines our global industrial economy. Without it, everything stops. If it's too expensive, the system can no longer expand.

Each barrel of oil (5.8 million BTUs) contains the energy equivalent of more than a decade of one human's labor.

That decade represents $400,000 in human wages, hence each $40 barrel of oil is the equivalent of $400,000 in human labor.

When oil hits $80 per barrel, that one barrel is the equivalent of $200,000 in human labor. No wonder the global economy sinks into recession when oil prices spike higher.

The fracking boom is an artifact of technology and cheap credit: without billions of dollars in cheap credit, the fracking boom would stop dead in its tracks. (Recall the fracking industry has lost $5 billion in the past few years.)

In effect, the Federal Reserve has subsidized fracking to suppress the cost of energy. Why? Because the incomes of the bottom 80% of households have stagnated for a decade. Since every product/service in the industrial economy requires energy, higher energy costs push the price of everything higher.

How can consumers maintain the high levels of discretionary spending the economy needs to sustain growth when costs are rising but their incomes are stagnant or declining when adjusted for inflation?

They can't.

Super-low interest rates also enabled households to fill the widening gap between their flat incomes and steadily increasing costs by borrowing: student loans, credit cards, auto loans, home equity lines of credit, etc. Many homeowners refinanced their mortgages at lower rates, lowering their payments and freeing up hundreds of dollars per month to fund additional consumption.

However, super-low interest rates mean super-low yields on safe investments such as Treasury bonds. Pension funds, insurers and other institutional owners of assets cannot meet their obligations if they earn 1%-2% annually (even less when adjusted for inflation). So the Fed's repression of yields has pushed these institutions and investors into risk-assets such as stocks, high-yield (junk) bonds and commercial real estate. In response, the Fed has backstopped risk assets with unprecedented purchases of assets – a term called Quantitative Easing. This has inflated bubbles in stocks, bonds and real estate as investors understood the Fed would never let assets drop, since any decline would wipe out pension funds, insurers, etc.

But these expedient policies have unexpected consequences.

Inflating assets has greatly widened wealth-income inequality, since only a relative few households and corporations own the majority of the risk-assets. Those who don't own meaningful amounts of these assets have lost ground while those who own the assets have seen their wealth skyrocket.

This has generated non-linear social discord, which has manifested political revolt (nationalism, etc.). As a result, central banks will no longer have the political leeway to bail out banks and the super-wealthy in the next financial crisis. The solution is to attempt to forestall such a situation from arising by maintaining the status quo so no crisis can ever erupt again.

But the boom generated by central bank stimulus has removed central banks' excuse for keeping interest rates low and buying assets. Now that the economy is growing smartly, interest rates should move higher and return to historic norms, and the Fed should reduce its balance sheet (selling assets instead of buying assets).

These moves will put the asset bubble at risk, since the fundamental drivers were 1) corporations could borrow cheaply and buy back their shares, pushing stock prices higher even as sales and profits flattened and 2) institutions and investors were driven into risk assets to earn a yield, i.e. chasing yields but at the cost of taking on much higher risks. Once yields rise, managers seeking to lower risk will sell risky assets in favor of safer assets.

Rising interest rates threaten to derail the fracking industry unless energy prices are allowed to rise.

Rising interest rates also increase the borrowing costs of households, reducing income available for the discretionary spending the economy needs to keep expanding.

All the money creation of the past decade has flowed into assets, inflating bubbles in stocks, junk bonds, housing and commercial real estate. These bubbles have pushed rents higher, as new owners need high rents to cover their costs. Easy credit has also enabled higher education to keep pushing costs higher, forcing students to borrow more to attend college.

Healthcare costs have also soared. Those exposed to rent, higher education, taxes and fees, childcare and healthcare are experienced inflation far above the official rate of 2% to 2.5%. By some measures, inflation is actually 7% to 10% annually for households in high-cost regions who must pay the unsubsidized costs of rent, higher education, taxes, childcare and healthcare.

These are the *unprotected households* exposed to the full impact of inflation.

Now interest costs are rising, too, adding another inflationary pressure.

In response to higher interest and ever-higher costs, those left behind are calling for *QE for the People*, i.e. central bank largesse should be distributed directly to households via Universal Basic Income (UBI), conventionally described as a $1,000 monthly stipend issued to every adult. The political class views UBI as politically expedient: since Fed-induced asset bubbles have pushed wealth inequality to the point of social instability, the easy fix is to borrow $2 trillion a year and distribute UBI to everyone.

Energy is the forgotten factor of inflation. If energy is abundant and cheap, new money flowing into the economy can boost productivity and output. This dynamic is not inflationary, as the pool of goods and services expands along with the money supply. But if energy is costly, new money isn't able to meaningfully increase productivity (hence our stagnating productivity as energy costs have risen). New money chases the existing pool of goods and services, pushing prices higher.

To summarize: cheap abundant energy, cheap goods and credit from overseas (globalization) and cheap abundant domestic credit funded by savings are non-inflationary.

Conversely, higher cost energy, rising costs of goods/credit from overseas, higher-cost credit domestically and vast injections of newly issued currency (i.e. UBI) are all inflationary.

Add these dynamics up and the only possible output is inflation that will start slowly but quickly accelerate to the point of severe financial pain and beyond.

In other words, the only way to maintain mass consumption as energy and other costs continue rising and ensure the mass of borrowers can service their expanding debts is to borrow or issue enormous sums of new currency and distribute it to the masses via QE for the People/UBI. The only possible output of these dynamics is inflation that gathers momentum as debt expands.

To counter inflation, central banks must push yields higher to attract capital to the newly issued debt. After all, what rational participant will buy a bond paying 3% when inflation is 10% annually? Nimble capital will flee risk assets in stocks, popping the asset bubbles, while the purchasing power of labor erodes even faster as inflation outpaces wage increases.

In response, the state must borrow increasing amounts to pay the higher interest costs on its ballooning debt and continue to fund QE for the People/UBI. The feedback pushes debt, prices and interest payments higher until the debt system collapses under its own weight: borrowers default, debts are forgiven or written off and sovereign state debt is devalued along with the state's currency.

Alternatively, should the issuance of debt be reined in, consumption will plummet and the economy will enter a self-reinforcing feedback loop of depression.

The keys to understanding the difference between the 1940s through the early 1970s (when expanding debt overcame stagnation) and the coming decade of non-linear disruption are the cost and abundance of liquid fuels and the decline of labor's value relative to speculative mobile capital.

The Keynesian/Modern Monetary Theory of borrowing and spending to optimize the productive capacity of the economy no longer aligns with the realities of the economy. These strategies will not just fail to achieve their desired results, they will actively accelerate the implosion of the entire system.

In effect, even now 80% of American households can no longer afford to consume enough and borrow enough to support a credit-based, high-energy consumption economy. The solution within the current status quo is to borrow stupendous sums to fund QE for the People/Universal Basic Income so households can continue to borrow and spend enough to keep the economy from entering a death spiral.

But creating currency is not the same as creating wealth, any more than keystrokes creating digital entries (i.e. new currency) is the same as creating more oil. The system is simply issuing more claims on the existing pool of energy and distributing debt in lieu of earned income. Issuing additional claims debases the currency being issued, reducing the purchasing power of all existing currency, i.e. inflation.

The Global Monetary Base has expanded 23-fold in just 32 years, from $800 billion in 1985 to $18.4 trillion in 2017. Inflation has remained tame for the past decade of rapid currency expansion, creating the illusion that issuing trillions in new currency and credit will never have any inflationary consequences. The only reason inflation has been limited is because of the deflationary effects of globalization, which pushed the costs of goods, services and capital lower.

But globalization, especially the emergence of China as a low-cost manufacturer, was a one-off. Now de-globalization is pushing prices higher via tariffs, nationalism, capital restrictions and higher labor costs in China and other emerging economies. The tailwinds of globalization have reversed into headwinds, and the only possible result of this change is higher inflation.

There is no other output of these dynamics other than currency debasement/inflation that is non-linear, where even modest changes can trigger non-linear crises. This is the point we are at now.

SECTION IV. The Non-Linear Potential of the Fourth Industrial Revolution

Over and above being a system of neofeudal extortion as described earlier, our economy is also undergoing convulsive non-linear changes powered by technologies that are obsoleting the cartels and institutions that enrich the entrenched elites—structures the elites expect technology to strengthen, not dismantle.

When Marx wrote that in a capitalist system, "everything solid melts into air," he was referring not only to the direct consequences of organizing production to maximize the expansion of capital—the dissolution of traditional economies, for example—but also to the second-order consequences: the disruption of family structures, etc.

In other words, when the structure of an economy is convulsed, so too are the social and political power structures.

The key attribute of any power structure is its innate resistance to any change which could threaten its power. Resistance to change turns any structure, no matter how well managed, brittle and thus fragile. The irony of this innate resistance to change is it is the source of failure: whatever cannot evolve and adapt becomes increasingly vulnerable to disruption.

Soaring wealth and income inequality is evidence that America's system is now rigged to benefit the entrenched few and their managerial elites. This system is increasingly vulnerable to decentralizing technologies that disrupt the highly centralized economic and social constructs that have been rigged to benefit the entrenched elites.

Due to the innate characteristics of centralized hierarchies, every nation-state's *power structure* is vulnerable to non-linear change, which can melt every social construct, no matter how vast or apparently secure.

In previous sections, we've covered the potential for non-linear dynamics to fracture social constructs that are not designed to withstand such forces.

But even if these brittle systems maintain their current stability, the confluence of technologies lumped into *the Fourth Industrial Revolution* introduce a mutually reinforcing set of dynamics that has the potential to obsolete much of the current economic structure, a non-linear process that will also melt social and political constructs into air.

Dynamics of the Fourth Industrial Revolution

An entire shelf of books could be written on these technologies, and due to the rapid evolution and hyper-coherence of these dynamics, the books would be out of date as soon as they were published.

I've assembled a list, by no means exhaustive, that touches on a few of these dynamics. In the interest of brevity, I am sketching the outlines of complex topics that I invite you to explore in greater depth.

1. A new mode of production

The phrase *mode of production* encompasses the entire productive machinery of an economy's output: its technologies, energy sources, financial structure, social constructs, political organization, value system, and so on. In broad-brush, the current mode of production is exemplified by a supply chain of mass-produced goods that flow from China/Asia and elsewhere to distribution points in the U.S., or globally sourced parts delivered to assembly points. A vast distribution system then delivers the goods to consumers or retailers.

The most profitable aspects of this mode of production are finance (credit), leveraged speculation and distribution of goods and services. These are largely controlled by global corporations based in the U.S.

The government—federal, state and local—regulates this mode of production and collects taxes which fund its social-welfare redistributions and spending on governance, national defense, etc. Both the public and private sectors of this mode of production depend on a permanent expansion of debt (borrowing) to sustain spending. In this mode of production, price is presumed to be the arbiter of value and the prime motivator: the goal is to maximize private gain by whatever means are available.

The Fourth Industrial Revolution:
- isn't simply the extension of existing technologies such as software and robotics; it is also includes new social and political values and structures. For example, the value of localizing production (e.g., the value of local food production and distribution under the banner of *food security*) extends

beyond price: the cost of imported food might be lower but the local production and distribution is more highly valued than price alone.
- enables localized production via 3D fabrication of many products. This capacity doesn't obsolete all mass-produced centralized production, but it reduces dependence on centralized production and global supply chains.
- isn't just re-ordering the mode of production; it's also re-ordering the creation and distribution of capital and profits. These changes are non-linear, meaning that adoption may be very gradual at first and then suddenly old models crumble and new ones arise in a very short time.

2. New social organizational tools

The established social/tribal forms such as political parties are losing their hold as social media and the Internet enable a much broader range of social identities, groups/tribes and membership.

3. Limits on growth and consumption

The current mode of production is organized around optimizing growth of production, credit, and consumption. There are limits to all three on a finite planet. The concept of DeGrowth—valuing sustainability above growth—is integral to the new suite of values.

4. Profits decline in a commoditized global economy

Value/profit is a function of scarcity and demand. When everything from credit to labor to components to goods and services is commoditized (i.e. interchangeable regardless of source), the scarcity value of everything (including intangible capital such as intellectual property) drops to near zero, and profit margins follow.

5. Profits from finance and globalization have peaked and are in an S-Curve decline

Dynamics of everything from the spread of contagious diseases to the financial gains of globalization trace out what's known as the S-Curve: a brief period of rapid growth is followed by a maturation phase that tops out and decays into decline. Credit expands until the qualified buyers have been exhausted; credit is then issued to unqualified borrowers who soon default, triggering the collapse of the entire credit cycle.

The benefits of globalization—labor arbitrage, lower cost components, etc.—have also peaked as national interests and the rapid rise of costs in developing economies extinguish further cost cutting.

6. Ordinary labor and capital, credentials and workers with credentials are all in over-supply

Whatever is in over-supply has no scarcity value. This includes ordinary labor (credentialed or not), ordinary capital, most credentials and workers with credentials, which have lost their *signaling value*. (A university diploma signaled the student's ability to stay the course and navigate a bureaucracy, hence his/her readiness to work in a corporate or government bureaucracy. Whether the student actually gained any knowledge is immaterial to the signaling value of the credential. Needless to say, in a knowledge-based economy this is a bankrupt concept and system.)

7. Conflicts between new and old elites

The conflict between new and old elites is as old as politics, and is a primary driver of modern finance-capitalism. New elites may not support the existing power structure, and the foundation of their wealth may actively dismantle the sources of old elites' wealth and power. Just as the Old Elite in England that derived its wealth from land was replaced by the New Elite whose wealth flowed from industrialization in the late 19th century, New Elites have arisen from software and digital technologies that are displacing Old Elites whose wealth flowed from the FIRE sectors (finance, insurance and real estate).

8. Centralization vs. localization and decentralization

One manifestation of this trend is cryptocurrencies, which are intrinsically decentralized and tailor-made for localization of finance, production and consumption.

The centralized model organizes everything in a top-down hierarchy in which cooperation is ordered by centralized authority. In a decentralized model, independent, localized nodes in a loosely bound network cooperate and collaborate without being controlled by a central authority.

9. The limits of old models

The old models of central bank stimulus via the purchase of assets and Keynesian fiscal stimulus have failed to restart organic growth, i.e. growth that isn't dependent on gargantuan monetary-fiscal stimulus. The model of increasing regulations and complexity is also failing to deliver improvements, while the costs of compliance soar. Increasingly elaborate schemes to maintain the Status Quo are piling up trillions of dollars in additional costs just to keep the system glued together.

10. Asymmetry between winners and losers drives conflict between markets and democracy

Democracy requires transparency, inquiry, skepticism, testing of hypotheses, and an open competition of ideas and critical thinking. The financial winners have purchased political influence while the losers have been disenfranchised. Democracy has been reduced to a public-relations façade cloaking entrenched interests.

11. Post-consumer society

Consumption does not generate a positive social role, i.e. a positive identity, purpose and meaning; only production and participation yield positive social roles. Thus consumer-based solutions such as Universal Basic Income fail to substitute for work and social structures based on contributing time and labor and making shared sacrifices. I explain this in detail in my book *Money and Work Unchained*.

12. Resistance to "expertise" and the power of the Managerial/Technocrat class

The obedience to authority resting on expertise is decaying as the global citizenry come to understand that expertise is bought, sold and packaged for consumption like any other good or service: corporations, think tanks, etc. hire experts to justify self-serving policies under the guise of disinterested science. This expertise-in-service-of-elites is eroding the authority that the managerial class took as its birthright.

13. Protected cartels are being obsoleted

What is efficient, profitable and productive will replace what is inefficient, stagnant and costly. The technology to fabricate medications might become ubiquitous, for example, destroying much of the scarcity value and political power of Big Pharma. Institutions act as *behavioral and capital sinks*: they suck up power, labor, income and capital, leaving less for innovation and adaptation.

14. Capital/talent magnets, artificial scarcity and overcoming entrenched elites

Open societies that aren't dominated by neofeudal extortion rackets and sclerotic centralized bureaucracies will attract capital and talent. Capital and entrepreneurial talent follow the lowest-cost, lowest-friction pathways to systems that protect property, legal and labor rights and a level playing field.

Entrenched elites seek to protect the artificial scarcity value of their goods, services, capital and authority. This protection is particularly dangerous because this stifles competition and the free flow of capital, labor, ideas and best practices, sapping the entire system of vitality, variability, talent and adaptability, the very traits the system needs to survive non-linear changes.

Entrepreneurial talent must tear down all the barriers erected by existing neofeudal elites to gain the freedom needed to create new value. Once the artificial scarcity imposed by existing elites is broken, the income, wealth and political power of existing elites will also be broken. No wonder the entrenched elites will fight so desperately to maintain the neofeudal system that protects their wealth and power!

In terms of implementing a National Strategy, it boils down to a simple, profound choice: those nation-states that enable entrenched elites to protect the scarcity value of their goods, services, capital and authority at the cost of flexibility and adaptability become brittle, fragile and extremely vulnerable to mutually-reinforcing non-linear dynamics. In a word, they are primed to collapse.

15. Mass Unemployment/Underemployment

Another potential non-linear dynamic unleashed by the Fourth Industrial Revolution is mass unemployment or under-employment as the rising costs of labor and labor overhead (healthcare, disability insurance, etc.) drive employers to automate every task that can be profitably automated, displacing human labor.

There are two dominant schools of thought on the potential decline of paid work: the first holds that technology always creates more jobs than it destroys, and the solution is to train workers to create higher-level value with their labor.

The second school holds that human labor will be permanently displaced, but since robots are inherently profitable, we can pay tens of millions of unemployed people Universal Basic Income so they will be free to become poets, entrepreneurs, filmmakers, etc.

I debunk both schools in my book *Money and Work Unchained*. In brief: job statistics are unambiguous: training more students in technology (STEM, science, technology, engineering and math) or STEM plus art (STEAM) has not created millions more jobs in technology. Rather, it has over-produced elites, one of Turchin's three causes of social disintegration: highly educated workers comprise an elite that has been implicitly promised secure, highly paid positions. Issuing 10,000 diplomas in chemical engineering does not magically create 10,000 positions for chemical engineers; there is only so much demand for STEM or STEAM graduates.

In addition, automation is eating its way up the value-creation food chain, replacing skilled workers as well as unskilled.

As for the belief that robots produce immense profits: this is also false, since robots are commodities, i.e. they are increasingly interchangeable, and therefore they generate no durable scarcity value or profits. If Company A can replace human labor with a mass-produced robot, so can Company B. The competitive advantage of reducing human labor by buying robots is lost as Company B can lower its prices and take market share from Company A. Company A will have to match the lower prices and so whatever savings were generated by buying commodity robots don't become profits.

Value flows to what's scarce. If robots are mass-produced tools anyone can buy, they cannot generate scarcity value, i.e. big profits.

What few (if any) conventional economists examine is the dispensable nature of much of the paid work in advanced economies, work that qualifies as *BS work*: jobs that process unproductive complexity masquerading as value-creation.

This can be tracked by comparing the number of additional tenured professors hired by the higher education sector in the past decade (few) and the number of compliance/complexity functionaries added to administrative staffs (many). The same is true of healthcare: the number of administrative positions added dwarfs the number of physicians and nurses added.

BS work adds nothing to the actual processes of education or healthcare; these tasks serve complexity, not output, and as such they will be the first to disappear when non-linear dynamics disrupt unproductive complexity. The higher the organization's inefficiency and complexity, the greater the gains to be reaped by eliminating unproductive complexity.

Put another way: BS work in service of unproductive complexity is increasingly unaffordable and therefore increasingly vulnerable to systemic disruption. What is unsustainable will vanish.

It's not difficult to imagine how this will occur; we need only look at informal economies that arise when currencies are debased to near-zero. Teachers, doctors and nurses are paid in cash or equivalent, and the immense top-heavy structures of billing, regulations, compliance, enforcement, advocacy and adjudication all vanish: there's no longer any money to pay people to generate low-value complexity.

Those who have never been employers—the vast majority of people—lack the experience needed to understand that hiring an employee entails great risk and liability, and no employer will hire an employee unless the employee can generate substantial value above their wage, as the employer must pay all the labor overhead (healthcare, workers compensation, disability and unemployment insurance, etc.), the general overhead of the enterprise (rent, utilities, fees, taxes, etc.) and still reap a profit to enable reinvestment, replacement of aging equipment, etc.

The net result is the market can only create jobs if enterprises are highly profitable and can become even more profitable by expanding. In a stagnating economy, very few businesses qualify.

As for the state hiring millions of unemployed: the state relies on tax revenues from the employed and profitable enterprises, and in a stagnant economy, the number of employed and profitable businesses both decline, leaving a smaller base for the state to tax. The only other source of revenues is to increase taxes or borrow money, a process that adds interest expense without necessarily expanding the future tax base needed to pay the higher interest.

The point here is that neither the market nor the state has the incentive or the ability to pay millions of unemployed people unless opportunities to reap profits that require human labor are abundant and tax revenues are rising. The faith that the market will always create tens of millions of new jobs is just that, a matter of faith, as is the notion that the state can pay tens of millions of unemployed people by borrowing trillions of dollars even as the economy that funds the state stagnates.

Another unexamined result of systemic unemployment is the loss of *positive social roles*, a subject I examine in great depth in my book *Money and Work Unchained*. Humanity is a social species, and every individual wants to be valued, to participate, to contribute, to be needed and to earn the dignity of contributing to the common good. People naturally want to improve their situation, and distributing *Bread and Circuses* (Universal Basic Income) doesn't create positive social roles or offer avenues to contribute or be needed.

Magical thinking about the Fourth Industrial Revolution is appealing because we naturally avoid facing problems that can't be solved by the status quo. As Krishnamurti observed, *"It is not the unknown we fear, but the known coming to an end."*

Neither the market nor the state can solve chronic unemployment. We need a third system that isn't enslaved by the tyranny of profits or borrowing money to fund BS work.

SECTION V. The Geopolitical Context of a Non-Linear World

Whichever nation-states survive the disruption of their existing modes of production will have geopolitical power simply by being one of the few that sacrificed its entrenched elites fast enough and early enough to adapt successfully in a tumultuous non-linear environment.

As noted in the previous section, value flows to whatever is scarce and in demand. If we refer to Maslow's Hierarchy of Human Needs, we can start with fresh water, food, shelter, and energy, and a system to distribute these essentials to the populace. Despite the apparent abundance of these essentials in much of the world, they are intrinsically scarce, as they require sustained investment and maintenance. Absent sustained effort, focus and sacrifice, these essentials go away.

Freedom of movement, agency, labor and capital are also intrinsically scarce, as they require an institutionalized set of specific social values and a political infrastructure to limit exploitation, extortion and predation. These freedoms also require sustained effort, focus and sacrifice.

Low-cost, low-friction pathways for capital, knowledge and talent (*ease of flow*) in self-organizing, decentralized, fast-evolving networks are also scarce, as they can only exist in economies where elites are unable to impose artificial barriers to entry and scarcities to protect their income, wealth and power.

Nation-states dominated by centralized power structures cannot limit the power of elites, because the cost of influencing (or corrupting) the elites is always much lower than the profit potential of imposing artificial scarcity.

Nation-states that offer broad-based access to these intrinsically scarce essentials and intangible social capital are thus also intrinsically scarce. Only decentralized nation-states are structured to limit elites from imposing artificial scarcity, as trying to influence many nodes in a decentralized network is much more difficult than influencing just one node in a centralized network.

Centralized hierarchies are by their very nature hyper-coherent, where authority issues commands to every official and agency. Hyper-coherence is beneficial in linear eras but dangerous in non-linear eras, as failure quickly cascades through the system.

Nation-states that survive as political entities but that no longer offer broad-based access to the scarce tangible and intangible essentials listed above will not attract capital or talent. Instead, they will bleed capital and talent as the most ambitious will flee for climes that encourage their flourishing.

Nation-states that have surpluses of food and energy will have leverage over those nation-states that do not have surpluses of food and energy. Dependence on other states for essentials is another form of hyper-coherence: shortages quickly cascade through global markets. Only states that are largely self-sufficient in essentials (i.e. autarkies) will avoid the cascading crises of hyper-coherent global markets.

Nation-states that generate surpluses of essentials and productive capacity will have the means to invest in building alliances, protecting trade routes and other forms of power projection. Nation-states that offer low-cost, low-friction flows of capital, knowledge and talent in self-organizing, decentralized, fast-evolving networks will attract the capital and talent needed to strengthen adaptability and the production of what is scarce.

Nation-states that depend on issuing new currency and debt to fund their brittle, elite-dominated domestic economies and governments will find the purchasing power of their currency and the value of the debt being issued will plummet to near-zero in non-linear fashion, despite the assurances of Modern Monetary Theory economists that there are no upper limits on currency issuance, borrowing or state spending.

The number of nation-states that have the capacity and willingness to jettison their existing power structure and entrenched elites is very likely zero. In this scenario, there are no successful strategies, there are only spasmodic, politically expedient grabs of whatever is still within reach.

The non-linear world I have sketched out is incomprehensible to the elites complacently ensconced in the current status quo. They are no different from the Ming and Roman elites who gazed at the immense power of the empire around them and reckoned it to be permanent, regardless of the challenges and weaknesses that were obvious to all but the self-deluded.

A decade hence, all lay in ruin.

We stand on the crumbling precipice of non-linear change. Those who want a national strategy that isn't just a jumble of magical thinking must first understand the need to completely transform the domestic economy and society into a resilient, sustainable foundation—a decentralized, adaptable foundation that will be uniquely scarce in a world of collapsing neofeudal power structures.

SECTION VI. The Failure of Status Quo Responses

The Limits of Force

The primary role of the state is to maintain order, and the primary tool of maintaining order is centralized hierarchy, i.e. bureaucracy, led by a professional managerial elite, i.e. technocrats. Centralized power in the hands of technocrats enables a swift, comprehensive response to disorder, as the state wields the authority to enforce obedience and compliance.

The response of political and financial authorities to the financial crisis of 2008-09 is a recent example of this model in action. Order was quickly restored by the directives of central bank and state authorities to limit market mechanisms and provide essentially unlimited liquidity to financial institutions.

This model of wielding state authority to restore order without waiting for the slow wheels of representational governance to turn has a long history. In the modern era, the Depression and World War II provide many examples, from the outlawing of private ownership of gold (seen as a dangerous form of hoarding when the state wanted the citizenry to spend, spend, spend) to the mass imprisonment of Japanese-American citizens, to the numerous executive orders establishing secret agencies with few limits on their power.

As anyone who is familiar with Nassim Taleb's work understands, this use of force to restore order may be successful in the short-term, but long-term stability depends rather ironically on a systemic tolerance for the disorder that comes with flexibility, variability, experimentation and dissent—all the traits of adaptability and resilience.

Power can be a heady elixir that fosters a very attractive illusion of control in those wielding it. The ability to force disorder into order by diktat encourages a dangerous confidence that any crisis can be handled by managerial elites wielding vast authority.

But systemic failures exacerbated by non-linear dynamics can't be resolved by diktat or force. A sudden oil embargo (as in 1973) can be countered with forced rationing, but this this doesn't resolve the fundamental flaw in the model of infinite expansion of consumption. Similarly, brute-force bail-outs of private institutions in 2008-09 did nothing to address the fundamental failings of a financialized, speculation-driven economy or the swallowing of democracy by neofeudal wealth.

Instead, these restorations of order at the expense of the disorderly dynamics of adaptability only increased the brittleness and vulnerability of the status quo. The disorder of the Global Financial Meltdown was symptomatic of a broken system. Force restored surface order--but this treated the symptoms, not the underlying disease.

Should civil disorder arise from the decline of social mobility and extremes of wealth inequality, the authorities will restore order by calling up the National Guard. But this restoration of order via brute force will do nothing to address the underlying sources of disorder.

As Taleb has explained, sustainable stability requires disorderly bubbling of variability, experimentation, dissent, and the redistribution of power so these adaptations can take root rather than be marginalized or suppressed by institutions fixated on maintaining the status quo by force.

It's instructive to recall Edward Luttwak's distinction between *force* and *power* in his book *The Grand Strategy of the Roman Empire* where he defines force as a mechanical input (expense) that doesn't scale; it takes a lot of people, effort and treasure to force others to comply with authoritarian edicts. Power, on the other hand, reflects the total output of the nation-state: its productive capacity, resources, human and financial capital, social mobility and cohesiveness, shared purpose—everything.

Technocrats take their authority to force compliance as power, but real power attracts cooperation; it has little need for force. Brute-force diktats to maintain a surface stability of order only increase the brittleness and fragility of the system. This is the false promise of authority: we can force stability by forcing compliance. But sustainable stability is the output of adaptability, i.e. *productive disorder*, not force.

The Appeal of the Enlightened Dictator

Following close on the heels of the illusion that authority to force compliance is the solution to non-linear crises is the strong appeal of the *Enlightened Dictator*—the clear-sighted individual with dictatorial powers who can force the needed changes (and sacrifices) down the resistant throats of those who are incapable of bold action on their own.

The stereotypical *Enlightened Dictator* in the corporate world was Steve Jobs, famously dictatorial, clear-sighted, and bold enough to strip the bloated, overly complex, ineffective and insolvent carcass of Apple Computer down to a unified structure overseen by a very lean management team. Summarily cashiering thousands of employees was just one of the steps that was taken out of dire necessity.

In the political realm, President Franklin D. Roosevelt issued such sweeping Executive Orders that many would reckon him (and other presidents as well) as democracy's equivalent of the Strongman.

The fallacy of the Enlightened Dictator arises from the confusion between very different types of crises. A profit-maximizing corporation that makes consumer products is a very specific form of organization. This type of enterprise must have products consumers want to buy and it must sell those products at a profit, net of all expenses, taxes, research and development and dividends paid to shareholders. If the enterprise fails to make products consumers want, or fails to make a profit on those sales, the resulting losses will eventually bankrupt the company and it will cease to exist.

This is a simple system with a simple set of goals compared to an economy or a society, and it is not a democracy. The owners of the company (shareholders) elect a board which selects the chief executive officer and senior managers. Such an enterprise is *opt-in*: consumers have a choice to buy the products, employees can choose to quit, and shareholders can sell their shares. This opt-in structure and the hierarchy simplify management: anyone management doesn't want to keep are let go, and any who don't want to be involved leave of their own accord. Everyone is to some degree a willing participant.

Contrast this to crises in sprawling economies and societies, which can be temporary or systemic (long-term). A decisive leader (some version of an Enlightened Dictator) may well resolve a temporary crisis with bold action, but systemic problems such as the decline in social mobility, skyrocketing wealth-income inequality and the emergence of pay-to-play governance (nominally a democracy but an oligarchy in practice) are not fixable with a few bold diktats. Such systemic crises require changes in the power structure of the economy and society, a redistribution of access to capital and political influence, and a reworking of the system's incentive structures.

Lastly, highly centralized organizations such as corporations and central banks can push down diktats because there are relatively few nodes in the system. When financial authorities bailed out banks in 2008-09, the number of affected financial institutions was small: a handful of Federal Reserve banks extended lines of credit to a handful of money-center banks, insurance companies and foreign banks.

Crises such as the stagnation of labor's share of the economy and the decline of social mobility cannot be solved by short-term emergency diktats. To solve systemic crises, the source of the crises—the very structure of our economy and society—must be reworked.

The fantasy that an Enlightened Dictator can solve all our systemic crises appeals to us for the same reasons borrowing more money appeals to us: they're both expedient and don't require fundamentally reordering the power structure.

Masking Failure with Propaganda

Let's recall the two contexts established at the start of this book: evolutionary principles and system dynamics. It doesn't matter who is in power, what political party holds power, or what form of governance holds sway: brittle, maladaptive systems will decay and collapse once they encounter cascading non-linear upheavals. Global reach and power will not save maladaptive systems, any more than its global reach and power saved the Western Roman Empire from collapse.

The response of centralized institutions to their structural failure is to hide their failure from public view and invest heavily in public-relations signaling that all is well. Behind these screens, the institutions continue to do more of what's failed because insiders are unwilling to make the sacrifices required to change the institution's optimization and output. They see no reason to suffer pain when it's so expedient to 1) hide the failure from public view; 2) project the illusion of success by public-relations signaling (promoting heavily laundered statistics, etc.); or 3) borrow more money.

Institutional leadership that pursues any of these three expediencies is admitting that the institution is unwilling and/or unable to make the sacrifices needed, and that the leadership is either unaware or in denial that this inability dooms the organization to decay and collapse.

A classic institutional response is to launch a study of the problem and then declare victory by issuing a new policy statement that includes all of the key concepts of adaptation as empty buzzwords, an elaborate show of transformation to mask the lack of real transformation.

Another classic response is a public-relations blitz constructed around misleading *signals of success*. In the financial realm, the classic signal that all is well is a rising stock market. So central bank and Treasury authorities have pushed the stock market higher for a decade (as of this writing in November 2018) to signal the public that the economy is thriving and those in authority are doing a great job.

In similar fashion, failing school boards cherry-pick positive student scores, Pentagon officials cherry-pick positive test results of failing weapons systems, and so on, in a nearly infinite flood of manufactured, gamed or laundered signals of success designed to mask the abject failure of the institution.

The past success of masking failure encourages authorities to invest even more heavily in PR signaling while the institution continues to do more of what's failed.

The Soviet Union also went to extraordinary lengths to generate the PR illusion of success and prosperity. But this strategy of persuading people that failure is success is akin to telling a hungry person that since others report being full, they should feel full, too. It is a strategy that signals a deep, systemic failure, and eventually people catch on that it's all artifice designed to mislead them.

Too Big to Fail is now an article of faith in the U.S. The leadership of vast agencies and institutions are convinced that even though entire empires—most recently, the Soviet Union—have collapsed, American institutions are immune to consequence, regardless of their failure. This faith is based on the idea that the U.S. can always issue as much money as is needed to paper over failure. But as we shall see next, this comforting faith is not reality-based.

Currency Debasement

The implicit American solution to systemic failure is *print our way out of trouble*, i.e. issue however many trillions of new dollars are needed to paper over the crisis. The success of this solution in the 2008-09 Global Financial Meltdown has strengthened the faithful's belief that the

Federal Reserve and the Treasury can create or borrow however many trillions are needed with no consequence to the stability of the system.

Since the U.S. dollar is a global reserve currency (that is, a currency other nation-states hold as reserves against trade imbalances and crises in their own currency), the dynamics of the dollars are complex. Nonetheless the basic concepts are not complicated. Currencies are valued, like every other market, by supply and demand. Value flows to what's scarce and in demand, and drains from what's abundant and not in demand.

Dollars created out of thin air by the Federal Reserve as well as dollars borrowed into existence by private-sector banks enter the asset markets of stocks, bonds and real estate. These new dollars chase a limited pool of stocks, bonds and real estate (assets), and the net result is rampant asset inflation. For example, a house that sold for $140,000 in 1998, may now be worth more than $900,000 in some areas of the country, though it provides no additional value as shelter to its residents. The increase in the price is entirely driven by the flood of new money seeking gains in asset markets.

According to official measures of inflation, which understate actual inflation for the unsubsidized and unprotected, the reason real-world inflation has been tame is because very little of this new money has trickled down to the real-world economy other than student loans, auto loans and credit card debt, which collectively make up only a modest part of the economy.

But once money is created or borrowed into existence and pushed en masse into the real-world economy via Universal Basic Income or other forms of fiscal stimulus, the purchasing power of the currency will decline as a simple function of supply and demand. In effect, creating new currency is like adding a zero to every bill. If every $1 bill becomes the equivalent of a $10 bill, what will happen to the price of an item that was $1? Absent other factors, the price will quickly rise to $10.

History shows that the expedient choice of every nation-state faced with crises that require reordering the power structure is to create more currency or reduce the intrinsic value of the money, which is essentially the same thing. By reducing the silver content of each coin, we can issue more coins...but each will be worth less. However, this expediency doesn't fool anyone for long, and prices rise accordingly, reducing the purchasing power of everyone holding the currency. This sleight-of-hand theft via inflation is a favored technique because it's a slow drip of loss rather than a dramatic loss that might arouse resistance.

The slow drip erodes purchasing power, and as people find their money buys less and less, the leadership's response is to issue even more currency, which only accelerates the erosion of purchasing power. Eventually people lose faith in the currency, and its value plummets in non-linear fashion. A recent example of this is Venezuela, once a wealthy nation but now impoverished by the collapse of its currency.

A variety of delusional beliefs support a complacent faith that the U.S. dollar could never suffer such a collapse of purchasing power. One is that the government can't go broke because it can always print as much money as it needs. As Venezuela has recently shown, printing currency with abandon isn't a solution, it's a greased slide to financial oblivion.

Others claim that since the dollars are borrowed into existence, the interest paid gives the currency a stable value. But if interest rates are rising, this is no longer the case.

Once the faith in the currency's value is lost due to expedient profligacy, rates must be raised to such high levels that interest payments bankrupt the government.

In other words, the comforting belief that the U.S. dollar could never suffer a non-linear decline in its purchasing power is simply that, a matter of faith. The faith that profligate issuance of currency has no consequences is based not on history but on magical thinking.

The core dynamic here is human nature. Insiders want to believe their expediency has no consequences, that the U.S. can survive essentially infinite institutional failure and financial profligacy without any adverse consequences. Since the alternative is painful sacrifices, this belief is as expedient as borrowing more money to fund *doing more of what's failed*.

These beliefs and dynamics ensure a non-linear collapse in the dollar's purchasing power within the next decade. No agency or institution will emerge from this currency crisis unscathed.

This cycle—avoiding sacrifice by issuing/borrowing more currency, and continuing to issue/borrow more currency even as the crisis deepens—cannot be reversed, as the pain of cold-turkey withdrawal only increases, and the cries of entrenched elites for more money rise exponentially.

No insider believes their share could possibly affect the great and mighty system; how can my fishing empty the sea? But tens of millions of people profligately overfishing can indeed collapse fisheries. The skeletons of once-great empires who reckoned they could finesse their way out of crisis by creating more currency litter the roadway of history.

The ultimate delusion is the belief that *it can't happen here*. The Ming and Roman officials thought that, too.

SECTION VII. Pathfinding a Sustainable Destiny

In discussing systems, it's easy to lose sight of the central issue: the survival or fall of our democratic republic (and by extension, all democratic republics). As we discuss the need for a third system beyond the market and the state, we're actually discussing the destiny of the nation.

A nation is more than political boundaries or its government. What binds people into a nation is not citizenship or force or dependence on the state; what binds people into a nation are shared ideals and shared purpose which incentivize sacrifices and effort on behalf of the common good.

The current system optimizes political corruption and neofeudal extortion. This structure is self-limiting; there is no way to prevent the failure of *business as usual*. But even if insiders manage to duct-tape the status quo together by increasing the public's dependence on the state via Bread and Circuses, that won't reverse the erosion of shared ideals and purpose. The government and political boundaries of the United States may remain as shell entities but the nation as a whole will have fallen.

When we discuss structures that optimize resilience, adaptability and sustainability, *we're discussing structures that are outside the status quo*. Be aware that insiders will incorporate these into their PR as buzzwords while continuing to do *more of what's failed*. Attempting to reform structures optimized to defend insiders is a waste of effort. The only way to change the nation's destiny is to obsolete the status quo by replacing it with new structures that are outside the control of global capital and the state.

Beyond the Market and the State

Insiders naturally hope that minor adjustments will be enough to weather any non-linear storm, regardless of its magnitude. The hope is that a meeting or two to strategize and a flurry of orders will be enough to transform the organization. This is wishful thinking, for all the reasons outlined earlier.

One fantasy after another is offered as a market or financial solution that doesn't require any real change in the status quo: "green" growth, borrowing and spending additional trillions, technological miracles (photovoltaic paint, etc.) and so on.

Insider reformers believe that existing structures and institutions can be transformed by adjusting the system's parameters, for example, increasing citizen oversight, adding art classes to STEM programs, and so on. Modest adjustments can generate modest increases in resilience and adaptability, but this is too little, too late when change becomes non-linear.

Outsider reformers believe that innovations can save the status quo: worker-owned collectives, the gig economy, artificially intelligent robots, etc. These may play a positive role, but they are limited by their reliance on the market and state.

The problem with all the proposed reforms is that they *leave the existing power structure and its perverse incentives intact*. If the power structure and perverse incentives remain as is, nothing of any importance has changed, and the system will produce the same dysfunctional, unsustainable output.

Even if insiders and institutions embrace the need for radical structural changes, few are willing to relinquish their power. Everyone will accept change as long as their position and pay remain unchanged.

The problem is existing organizations cannot be made resilient or adaptable because they are the *wrong structural type*. Being *the wrong unit type and size*, neofeudal organizations will cease to function once non-linear dynamics upend the status quo.

In effect, institutions are intrinsically incapable of adaptation when the first step requires dismantling the institution and the security of insiders. What insiders hope for is impossible: radical change that magically leaves the structure and their positions intact.

Consider higher education as an example. Student debt has doubled from $750 billion to $1.5 trillion in a few years; can it continue doubling every few years forever? Clearly, the system is unsustainable. What's needed is a system that *accredits the student, not the institution*, which effectively dispenses with the need for administration, student loans, and even the campus itself, where learning takes place wherever the undergraduate happens to be, or in the workplace.

A nearly free university (as outlined in my book *The Nearly Free University*) does not need a campus, a complex, or costly administration. It is essentially a software system that is easily replicated and customized to student needs and local conditions.

The same can be said of other self-organizing alternatives to maladaptive, neofeudal organizations.

The solution to absurdly unsustainable costs and institutional failure is to *obsolete the existing structure with a new structure that's outside the control of insiders*. It is unlikely that any existing institution will willingly dissolve itself as the first necessary step. Insiders will cling to the existing structure until it collapses.

To prevent the collapse of our democratic republic, we need *a new structure with new feedback loops that institutionalizes what will be exceedingly scarce in the coming non-linear era*: adaptability, resilience, wise use of resources, sustainability, *de-coherence* (loosely bound systems), decentralized governance, non-state currencies, self-sufficiency (autarky), DeGrowth (well-being without economic expansion), positive social roles, social mobility and shared purpose.

There's a useful phrase that encapsulates this National Strategy: *good ideas don't require force*. It's instructive to recall Luttwak's distinction between *force* and *power*: power influences others without coercion; it attracts cooperation. The successful National Strategy attracts capital, talent and cooperation not by forcing compliance but by enabling equal-opportunity access all that is scarce in a non-linear world. This is its source of power.

The successful National Strategy must shift the economy and society as follows:

- From optimizing the security of entrenched elites to optimizing the security of scarce essentials
- From unsustainable infinite expansion of consumption to sustainable DeGrowth/wise use of resources
- From brittle/fragile to resilient/adaptable
- From disintegrative/divisive to integrative/shared purpose
- From maximizing personal gain by any means available to a productive incentive structure
- From hierarchical authority to self-organizing networks
- From hyper-coherence to de-coherence/loosely bound systems

- From closed systems that optimize self-serving elites to open systems that optimize social mobility
- From centralization of capital and power to decentralization of capital and power
- From a focus on consumption to a focus on production *repair*
- From dependence on the state and other nations to agency and autarky (self-sufficiency)
- From centralized production to distributed production
- From waste and planned obsolescence to efficiency
- From reliance on debt to reliance on accumulating capital
- From concentrating wealth, income and power in the hands of the few to paid work and opportunities to build capital for all
- From maximizing extraction and profiteering (self-aggrandizement) to contributing to the common good
- From devoting capital to speculative gambling to addressing local scarcities
- From exploitation/free-riding to shared sacrifice
- From bureaucratic over-regulation/unproductive complexity to simple prescriptive guidelines
- From unaccountability/no skin in the game to accountability
- From neofeudal state/cartels to a local market/community economy

Insiders and reformers will claim *we can do all this within our existing market and state institutions,* but this is a magical-thinking fantasy for four reasons:

1) The market only provides capital and labor for profitable ventures; whatever isn't profitable is ignored;
2) The foundation of our system is an expansion of consumption funded by an expansion of credit, so any contraction in consumption or credit collapses the system;
3) The state-central bank system issues new money to those at the top of the wealth-power pyramid, ensuring the rich get richer because they alone have access to essentially unlimited cheap credit; and

4) Our current pay-to-play system of governance can be influenced for a fraction of the gains that can be reaped by those buying the influence.

Markets are blind to externalities (loss of biodiversity, etc.) and *social demand*, i.e. values that cannot be reduced to consumerist goods and services. These include positive social roles, self-sufficiency, local production, decentralized control of currency and capital, serving the common good and so on. As noted earlier, the market response to horrendous air pollution created by for-profit enterprises is to sell cans of fresh air. *Social demand* seeks the restoration of breathable air.

The neofeudal state-cartel system is defined by two intrinsic asymmetries: new money (credit) is available only to banks, financiers and corporations at the very top of the wealth-power pyramid, the top 1% of the economy. Those with access to low-cost credit can buy whatever political influence is necessary to secure their monopoly or cartel's profits for a fraction of the profits protected by the political influence.

The only possible outputs of our money-credit system are structural wealth and income inequality that converts to political dominance, and the debasement of the state currency. These asymmetries cannot be reformed; they are intrinsic to the structure of our financial and political systems.

The other core dynamic of the market and the state is *an illusion of choice*: consumer choices that serve the maximization of profit are presented as the *full spectrum of choice*, while the reality is *social demand* and *DeGrowth* are not on the spectrum of choice because neither serves the power structure or the market's core purpose, the concentration of capital and profits.

As for the state, candidates who serve the power structure are presented as the *full spectrum of choice*, while candidates that seek to replace the existing power structure never make it to the ballot. Bread and Circuses may be presented as changing the power structure, but that is illusion; distracting and placating the disenfranchised masses with Universal Basic Income/Bread and Circuses protects the power structure.

The only way to escape the status quo's *illusion of choice is to create a third system beyond the market and the state.*

We are left with a conclusion that many will find shocking: neither the market nor the state can resolve the problems outlined above, and neither are able to navigate the non-linear era we are entering. Both will fail spectacularly for all the systemic reasons explained above.

This will no doubt strike many as impossible because markets and state are all they've ever known, and so they assume these are the only possible systems. But markets and central states are *social constructs*, not natural systems. That these social constructs have dominated civilization for centuries doesn't mean they are some sort of physical law like gravity; they are simply a social construct that has run its course and has proven itself time after time to be incapable of sustainable resilience for all the reasons outlined in this book.

The only National Strategy with any chance of success is one that views non-linear dissolution of the status quo as an opportunity rather than a disaster. The core of this National Strategy is the development of a third system that institutionalizes everything that markets and the state cannot do.

This third system doesn't replace markets or government. It incentivizes our efforts to serve the common good rather than elites, and institutionalizes a set of principles and values that are not incentivized by the market or the state. I call this third system *the community economy*.

The Third System: The Community Economy

The only path to sustainable resilience is a *community economy* that's self-funded (i.e. not dependent on state funding or central bank credit) and that has the structure to address *social demand*, not just *aggregate (consumer) demand*.

Social demand isn't recognized in the current state-cartel system; the only demand that registers is consumer demand for profitable goods and services provided by the state. This is the fatal flaw of the current state-market system. It is entirely deaf to *social demand* for sustainable ways of living that may not be profitable, for positive social roles that contribute to the common good, for shared purpose and meaningful work. These are what people need and what's scarce, but the current market-state system lacks the incentives and structures to even recognize the scarcity, much less address it.

The most important needs beyond those of bare survival do not register in our state-market system; all human needs are reduced to consumerism and dependency on the state. That both the market and the state fail to fill social demand is blindingly obvious, yet because the system lacks the means to even recognize these needs, they simply don't exist in our system.

People quickly acclimatize to consuming less, borrowing less and becoming more efficient, but since there's little profit in a DeGrowth economy, the state will no longer able to operate at its current vast scale once economic activity withers.

And so the current market-state system is designed to fail not just its citizenry but humanity and the planet itself.

If there is no way to generate new credit and enormous profits, the current system implodes. A system hell-bent on generating stupendous profits by any means available optimizes waste, planned obsolescence, and marketing-driven demand for superfluous goods and services—all in the name of maximizing profits via the expansion of debt and consumption of resources, which are of course two sides of one coin: to buy the auto, house, college diploma, etc., the consumer needs credit.

In other words, human happiness has been distilled down to consumerism: the status quo insists the permanent expansion of goods and services is the primary driver of becoming happy. This distillation serves to maximize profits, not human happiness. In perverse ways, the current system precludes human happiness by its very structure.

The expansion of consumption funded by debt has created what my colleague Bart Dessart calls a *Landfill Economy* that profits from the wastage of resources into products engineered to fail and be unrepairable (planned obsolescence), ensuring that production ends up being discarded in the landfill, forcing the consumer buy new products.

This is the obsessive, counterproductive insanity of infinite *growth at any cost* on a finite planet.

The purpose of the community economy is to incentivize and institutionalize a set of sustainable values that isn't driven solely by profit, the expansion of credit or the protection of elites.

The core economic structure is the *community organization*, a highly flexible, voluntary (opt-in) self-organizing group whose goal is to fill specific local scarcities and provide *self-funded paid work* and positive social roles for all participants. This structure instantiates the core components of resilience and adaptability: decentralization, de-coherence, democratic governance, prescriptive guidelines, accountability, transparency, distributed (non-state) currency, variety, variability and wise use of resources (DeGrowth) in service of the common good and shared purpose.

Participants have equal opportunities to gain positive social roles, agency, self-reliance, income and to accumulate capital in all its forms: human, social, and tangible (financial, tools, etc.). Since good ideas don't require force, the community economy is entirely voluntary. People want to participate and contribute, and this system provides them multiple options to do so.

The essential characteristic of the community economy is its independence from the tyranny of the profit-maximizing market and the state's monopoly on issuing currency.

I describe this system in my book *A Radically Beneficial World*. My goal here is to distill the structural essentials of this adaptive, resilient system.

Centralization and Monopoly Optimize Corruption

If we set out to design a system that optimizes corruption, we'd ask, which one is easier to corrupt: a centralized system which concentrates power in one node, or a decentralized system of 1,000 roughly equal nodes?

The answer is of course the centralized system. We only need to influence a handful of politicians (all of whom must raise millions of dollars every election cycle to retain their power) to have a clause protecting our monopoly inserted in a massive spending bill. In comparison, influencing 1,000 smaller nodes would be extremely cumbersome, costly and time-consuming.

The default optimization of centralized power is thus corruption. This optimization is intrinsic to the structure itself, and has nothing do to with who is in office, or which party has power. This optimization isn't limited to electoral governance. The centralized power of regulatory agencies optimizes the revolving door between the middle-income regulators and the enormously wealthy corporations and banks they oversee. How else do we explain the regulators' refusal to investigate Bernie Madoff despite three documented appeals to do so over the span of many years?

If we wanted to lock in steady profits for our corporation, what's the lowest-cost, most reliable way to do so? Eliminate competition, and the lowest-cost, most reliable way to eliminate or limit competition is to lobby the state to erect high barriers to entry or institutionalize our monopoly or cartel, i.e. a monopoly with a handful of members.

The default optimization of the state-corporate system is monopoly. Once again, this has nothing to do with the particulars and everything to do with the structure of the state-corporate interface. The state is itself the ultimate monopoly, of course, retaining an absolute monopoly on the issuance of currency and credit and institutionalized regulation and use of violence (force).

The default optimization of monopoly is high profits, diminishing quality, near-zero accountability and transparency and the protection of insiders at the expense of outsiders. The few benefit at the expense of the many. This is of course the basic structure of criminal rackets and neofeudalism, which share the same structure of extortion.

How can we keep monopolies honest if there is no competition, accountability or transparency? The short answer is we can't, as monopolies/cartels concentrate wealth, and the centralized state concentrates power.

The only solution is decentralization of power, which flows from the issuance and distribution of currency.

The Essential Role of Non-State Currency

We have seen that the state's monopoly on issuing currency dooms the status quo to collapse all by itself, as the temptation to maintain the status quo by issuing more currency without regard to the consequences is irresistible. Therefore the one essential requirement of the community economy is a non-state currency which is issued by community groups as they produce goods and services in their communities, i.e. a *labor-backed currency*.

Such structural transformation will require painful sacrifices that few (if any) are willing to make unless everyone has to bear the same sacrifices. But since our current system *optimizes protecting insiders*, any and all sacrifices are structurally asymmetric. Insiders see no need to sacrifice when they can sacrifice the many to benefit the few.

Like the structure of the market and the state, the structure of our money and financial system are *social constructs* which serve the interests of those holding concentrated wealth and power. The only way to prevent the collapse of our democratic republic is to break the monopoly of the state (i.e. the central bank and Treasury) and private banks to issue currency and credit.

If we don't change the way currency and credit are created and distributed, we've changed nothing.

The only way to break the monopoly is to issue a competing currency which is which is independent of the state and banks and structured to retain its purchasing power. That is, the currency is not borrowed into existence and thus isn't a credit instrument, nor is it controlled by a centralized node (central bank) that serves the interests of political and financial elites.

As I explain in my book *A Radically Beneficial World*, the tools to create a decentralized currency already exist in the form of software and cryptocurrencies. The missing piece of the puzzle is a mechanism that ties together decentralized cryptocurrencies, meeting community scarcities and providing paid work for all participants. I outline such a system in the book: CLIME, the community labor integrated money economy.

The citizenry is best served by a host of competing currencies. This is the only way to *keep the state currency honest*. But just as importantly, the power to issue and distribute currency must be decentralized via embedding this power in the community economy.

Of all the steps needed to prevent the collapse of our democratic republic, the need for independent, decentralized non-state currencies is one of the most difficult for the average person to grasp. But once we understand that the power to issue and distribute currency and credit is the source of all political and financial power, then we understand why any reform that leaves the existing currency and credit system intact changes nothing.

The Structure of Resilience and Adaptability

It's easy to come up with a laundry list of characteristics of resilience and adaptability. The hard part is designing a *structure whose only possible output is resilience and adaptability*.

From the beginning of this inquiry, we've focused on understanding the *social constructs* of our economy and society as *systems* that are guided by the principles of natural selection—where, of the variations generated, the most beneficial traits are conserved—and systems dynamics. Every system is optimized to produce specific outputs by its structure and incentives. Our current system's default incentives are to conserve the existing structure and defend against anything that threatens the status quo's *power structure*.

We've also focused on *scarcity* as the driver of value, where monopolies maintain *artificial scarcities* that are enforced by the state to generate stable profits.

Hyper-coherence (tightly bound nodes), hierarchy (authority), centralization, suppression of dissent and monoculture are the dynamics of fragility and brittleness that *optimize failure* in non-linear eras.

Our neofeudal state-cartel system is structured to incentivize obedience and serving the interests of the few (insiders and elites). While the system claims to address scarcities, it has no mechanism to even recognize, much less address, the greatest scarcities in our system: for positive social roles, for shared purpose and broadly distributed rewards for serving the common good.

Instead, our system embraces the self-serving fantasy that the pursuit of narrow self-interest—maximizing profit by any means available and the accumulation of political power—magically serve the common good. As a result, the current system incentivizes profiteering, extortion and corruption.

The core processes of this social construct are *profit-maximizing growth of consumption at any cost* and *the profit-maximizing expansion of credit to enable that infinite growth*. The only possible output of this construct is a *Landfill Economy* that optimizes waste and planned obsolescence and a financial system that optimizes fraud, speculation, leverage and debt.

The status quo system is blind to the destructiveness and unsustainability of both processes. The system's sole goal is to sustain the insanity of infinite growth of consumption and credit for another quarter, another year, another election cycle.

The challenge is to design a system that institutionalizes (i.e. conserves and incentivizes) resilience and adaptability that serve social demands and scarcities, i.e. shared purpose and the common good.

Trust is an under-appreciated form of capital. Due to its reliance on propaganda to mask the asymmetric rewards of its neofeudal structure, the current system generates very little trust.

One of the great ironies here is the blindness of our state-cartel system to what's intrinsically scarce: trust, positive social roles, access to opportunities to belong, participate, contribute and accumulate capital by filling the scarcities in one's own community.

We currently inhabit a system bereft of both common sense and wisdom, a system that is blind to what's truly scarce and valuable while it busily hoards what it identifies as scarce and valuable—profits and political influence—for its insiders and elites.

Once the non-linear dynamics gathering on the horizon sweep over our absurdly short-sighted, hubris-drenched, greed-optimizing social constructs, everything that the insiders and elites consider so valuable—profits and political influence, and a structure that enforces their privileges—will melt into air, no matter how much force is applied.

Of the many self-serving delusions of our elites, perhaps none is greater than the delusion that *force is power*. As noted previously, true power attracts cooperation, talent, capital and the willingness to contribute and even sacrifice because power secures a trustworthy, difficult-to-corrupt, equal-opportunities-for-all structure with positive incentives to maintain all the traits that make the system resilient, adaptable and sustainable for all participants.

What dynamics define the structure of a resilient, adaptable system?

Optimizing Goals and Values

Reformers find it frustrating that ideals rarely find expression in status quo systems. The problem is existing systems optimize concentrating profit and power, and everything else is given lip-service. All human systems are social constructs, and all social constructs reflect goals and values that are institutionalized in incentives and the optimization of specific processes and outputs. As a general rule, existing systems embody *implicit* goals and values that may be at odds with the public-relations purpose.

If we want to institutionalize different goals and values—for example, a system that recognizes and responds to *social demand*—we must explicitly design the inputs, processes, incentives and feedback loops to generate the desired output. This is why reforming existing systems fails to change the output: the entire system will still generate output based on the previous goals and values that are counter to the reformers' idealization.

The solution is to design a new system from scratch whose only possible output is resilience and adaptability. In this section, we'll explore the dynamics that the new system must institutionalize.

De-Coherence and DeGrowth

Systems that are tightly bound (hyper-coherent) are exquisitely vulnerable to contagion of crisis and collapse. Resilience and adaptability are characteristics of loosely bound decentralized nodes (de-coherent). Any system that is dependent on monopolies or cartels (for example, *too big to fail* banks) is extremely vulnerable to collapse. Systems of loosely bound decentralized nodes are not dependent on any one single node; the system's diverse range of nodes and flexibility lends it redundancy and resilience. The breadth of its sources and processes are buffers against the failure of any one node.

Redundancy and buffers are not free. So while a monoculture corporate farm may generate cheaper outputs than a loosely bound decentralized system of 100 family farms, when a blight or pest wipes out the monoculture crop (or its corporate parent goes bankrupt in some financialization speculation), the true costs of stripping out redundancy and buffers will be revealed.

As noted above, it's much easier for an elite to buy control of one central node everyone is dependent on, and this vulnerability to elite dominance is intrinsic to centralized structures. The only structural defense against the dominance of self-serving elites is decentralization and de-coherence.

Those dependent on the monoculture corporate farm will fail when it fails. Those dependent on the decentralized system of 100 family farms will find the failure of a single node, or even a handful of nodes, will not collapse the entire system.

De-coherence is served by a multitude of networked but independent nodes. Loosely bound networks are an ecosystem, not a monoculture.

The ultimate monopolies are state currency and central bank credit. The only structural defense against their eventual failure is decentralized redundancy, i.e. a multitude of currencies and sources of credit which are independent of each other.

Structures that institutionalize independence from monopolies and monocultures are *scarce social constructs and thus of great value*. The value of being free of the tyranny of dependence does not even register in a structure optimized to maximizing profits. Systems that conserve de-coherence are optimized for social and financial resilience and adaptability. Structures that institutionalize resilience and adaptability are also *scarce social constructs and thus of great value*.

Structures that optimize efficiency and wise use of resources (i.e. DeGrowth) are also *scarce social constructs and thus of great value*, as opposed to our current social construct (market-state) which optimizes *growth at any cost and the Landfill Economy on a global scale.*

There is no structural reason why humanity can't live well on a fraction of the energy and resources we squander in the current *infinite growth of consumption and credit system*. The dependence on infinite expansion of consumption and credit is a consequence of the insane social construct we currently inhabit. We are blind to what's structurally scarce and valuable because *social construct scarcities* don't even register. Trapped inside insanely unsustainable systems, we can't see what's truly scarce and valuable: structures that institutionalize sustainable resilience and adaptability.

The only way to institutionalize DeGrowth is to institutionalize incentives and structures that *optimize doing more with less* by paying participants for decreasing consumption of resources and increasing efficiency in service of the community's common good. The only way to pay participants for what may well be intrinsically unprofitable work is to de-couple the currency being issued from profit and from credit, and the only way to do this is to empower each qualifying node of the community economy network to issue currency for work that addresses scarcities and social demand in each node's community.

The community economy institutionalizes an ethos of sustainability by accepting material limits, optimizing the extraction of the most social value from energy and resources, and offering meaningful employment and opportunities to build capital to everyone who chooses to participate. This structure institutionalizes the filling of local social demand which serves the common good. As a result, it also institutionalizes shared purpose.

Prescriptive Guidelines and Goals

Centralized hierarchies control those within by enforcing obedience to enormously complex regulations. Centralized hierarchies optimize rigid chains of command and rigid processes defined by detailed regulations. The *agency* (ability to think and act independently) of those in the hierarchy is de-optimized, as independent thought and action are threats to the entire system of control.

As the hurricanes of non-linear dynamics tear these centralized structures apart, those at the top will issue orders to *do more of what's failing*, i.e. follow rigid regulations that no longer make sense. As noted previously, obedience is a self-selected trait of those inside these structures, because those who wanted agency already quit or were pushed out.

As we have seen, obedience to a rigid regulatory structure optimizes linear stability. In non-linear instability, these brittle structures fail, and workforces optimized for obedience to complex regulations are poorly equipped to manage disruption. Resilient structures rely not on hierarchies and enforced obedience to rigid regulations but on *prescriptive goals and guidelines*, goals and general guidelines that instantiate productive incentives and values but that leave the details up to those performing the work. Prescriptive guidelines only work in structures that enforce accountability and transparency, where failure generates corrective feedback that cannot be ignored or buried.

Consider the governmental issuance of a permit for some activity. In the current structure, a complex set of regulations and steps must be processed through a chain of command, and compliance requires a great deal of time and resources. The system optimizes obedience and compliance, and the benefits generated by speedy, cost-effective issuance of permits are de-optimized; they don't register or count. Delays and inefficiencies are considered *the cost of doing business*.

Conversely, in a prescriptive system, the structure is broken down into competing teams and a queue of applicants. Those teams which issue permits expeditiously are rewarded accordingly. The prescriptive goal is: issue 80% of all permits within one day. The prescriptive guidelines are equally general: protect the public from avoidable risks and maximize serving the common good. How each team manages the goals and guidelines is up to them. The input, process and output are transparent and available for anyone to review, so corner-cutting or favoritism will be visible to all participants.

In education, a prescriptive system would offer all students a choice of teams tasked with simple goals and guidelines: *every student will be taught how to learn on their own, up to and including the most challenging subjects*. How each team meets this goal is up to them. Since the inputs, process and output are all transparent and available to all participants, students will choose to join the teams that prove most successful in teaching students to learn on their own. Teams that underperform will have no students and will disband.

Prescriptive systems are natural selection in action: variations that benefit adaptability and resilience are conserved and distributed, while those that detract from adaptability and resilience get selected out of the system and disappear.

Prescriptive systems require everyone to participate and accept responsibility (i.e. have skin in the game). Everything—inputs, processes and outputs-- is always on the table; nothing is sacrosanct or privileged. Prescriptive systems are scale invariant—they work in the same way regardless of the size or scale of the organization. Risk-taking is encouraged, as experimentation, sharing of results and curiosity are necessary to generate the variations that are the structural foundation of adaptability and resilience.

Self-Reliance and Self-Sufficiency

It is ironic that the status quo optimizes goals, values and dynamics that undermine adaptability and resilience, which are not deemed valuable in the current system. *Scarce social constructs don't even register in the status quo.* Conversely, the core goal of the community economy structure is to recognize and address social demand by institutionalizing decentralized, locally controlled social constructs that incentivize filling local scarcities of social demand.

In a world dominated by profit-maximizing mobile capital pursuing the infinite expansion of consumption, debt and centralized wealth and power (i.e. our current system), *social constructs that address social demand are scarce and thus valuable*. In other words, social constructs that optimize the maximization of profit by any means available and that concentrate wealth and power in the hands of the few are abundant and thus of little value.

In a similar fashion, structures that optimize dependence on monopolies and long supply chains that maximize profits are abundant and thus of little value.

Conversely, structures that optimize self-reliance and self-sufficiency (autarky) are scarce and thus of great value. Self-reliance and self-sufficiency are as a general rule immensely unprofitable. If I can fill my own scarcities myself, then my need to borrow money to consume more is very low, and thus my contribution to the status quo of infinitely expanding consumption and credit is low. The current system cannot sustain itself selling a single fishing pole to someone who then catches all their own fish. The status quo can only sustain itself if everyone is forced to buy more fish every week and do so using credit.

Government currently depends on tax revenues generated by transactions and the expansion of debt. People who are largely self-reliant and self-sufficient do not generate many transactions nor do they fund their minimal consumption with borrowed money. As a result, any widespread adoption of self-reliance and self-sufficiency will collapse the government.

The current system optimizes dependence on monopolies that fill endless consumer demand for credit, goods and services. The status quo thus optimizes a *Landfill Economy funded by ever-rising debt*. Social constructs that optimize a *Landfill Economy funded by ever-rising debt* are abundant and thus of little value. Government structures that depend on a *Landfill Economy funded by ever-rising debt* are abundant and thus of little value.

Decentralized, locally controlled social constructs that optimize self-reliance and self-sufficiency are scarce and thus of great value.

We are ceaselessly told that self-reliance and self-sufficiency are terrible because they reduce overseas trade and the expansion of consumption and debt, the lifeblood of the status quo.

Systems optimized for adaptability and resilience are *networked but independent*: resources needed to fill local social demand and local scarcities may well be imported from elsewhere, but since the goal isn't maximizing profit and monopoly (two sides of the same coin), reducing the need for scarce resources and credit are incentivized. This structure optimizes trade between community groups that is mutually beneficial cooperation, as opposed to the ruthless exploitation that is optimized by the existing system and called *free trade* for PR purposes.

Optimizing Agency and the Distribution of Income, Capital and Security

The existing system optimizes dependence on the state and private monopolies, and divesture of agency and capital controlled by the many into the centralized hands of the few. As a result, this system de-optimizes social mobility, agency and the broad distribution of capital and power.

The existing system thus optimizes *Bread and Circuses*, i.e. the implicit acceptance of divesting power and capital in exchange for the security of dependence on the state for such things as Universal Basic Income, which enables the mass consumption and debt service the system needs to sustain itself.

The community economy optimizes the broad distribution of agency and opportunities to accumulate capital—that is, the foundations of social mobility—by providing everyone with the opportunity to join a community group or start their own group. Since each group must agree to follow a structure of democratic governance, every participant has a say and a responsibility.

The foundation of capital accumulation is a secure income and equal access to intangible capital: knowledge, skills and social networks. The community economy offers every participant both a secure income (paid by currency issued by qualifying groups) and access to knowledge, skills and social networks.

The community economy optimizes agency by its opt-in structure. Everyone can choose to join a group, quit a group, or start a new group if they're dissatisfied with existing choices. Everyone has equal access to secure paid employment and opportunities to accumulate capital. (Outcomes of course are not equal. Differing inputs and processes will generate differing outputs.)

As explained in previous sections, democracy requires broadly distributed agency and capital. The existing system optimizes the erosion of democracy in favor of oligarchy. The community economy optimizes democracy by institutionalizing the universal opt-in opportunity to gain agency and equal access to secure income and opportunities to accumulate capital.

Structuring Accountability, Transparency and Democracy

Idealists are disappointed by the poor results of tweaking the parameters of existing systems. As noted previously, modifying parameters won't change the system. In a similar fashion, people won't change their response to incentives unless the incentives change.

Accountability (skin in the game), transparency and democracy are all easily thwarted in the current system, and the incentives embedded in the status quo encourage and reward the continual erosion of all three of these. There are currently few, if any, gains to be had by increasing accountability, transparency and democracy, and significant, mutually reinforcing gains to be had by decreasing them.

Accountability, transparency and democracy are intrinsically messy and costly, as they are the moving parts of inherently messy and costly adaptability and resilience. The human urge to mask failure and protect self-serving insider positions undermine compliance with any organizational attempts to enforce these traits, and centralized hierarchical organizations will eliminate these messy processes in favor of less messy technocratic obedience.

The solution to the self-serving introduction of unearned privilege and protection of insiders is to automate the processes of accountability, transparency and democracy via open-source software that is itself an instantiation of accountability, transparency and democracy. It's difficult to embed bias, unearned privilege and protection of insiders in open-source software that is open to inspection by all.

Corporate software systems that instantiate automated governance are ubiquitous. Participants who choose to join corporate systems are monitored by automated software that tracks their interactions and transactions for compliance and acts to correct rule-breakers. Corporate automated systems serve the corporation's ontological imperative to maximize profits by any means available, and so these systems are opaque to users.

Conversely, in the community economy, the automated governance software serves the common good by enforcing level-the-playing-field guidelines for participation and conduct, and doing so with transparent, open-source software that any participant can inspect or contribute to.

As I describe in my book *A Radically Beneficial World*, the democracy of community groups, their prioritization of local scarcities and social demand, their organization of the project and resources, and the issuance of currency to pay participants for their work can all be automated by software that is freely distributed and can be copied and used by new groups.

Institutionalizing Shared Purpose via Serving the Common Good

It's easy to give lip-service to abstractions such as shared purpose, but difficult to institutionalize shared purpose in the inherently messy real world. The key is to institutionalize an incentive structure that rewards serving the common good via filling local social demand and local scarcities, and de-incentivizes (by distributing warnings to those violating the rules that protect all participants from exploitation and predation and ejecting those who ignore warnings) bias, the establishment of unearned privilege and the protection of insiders from scrutiny and consequence.

In a global economy optimized to maximize profits and concentrate wealth and power, *decentralized, locally controlled social constructs that incentivize and institutionalize shared purpose by focusing effort and resources on serving the common good are scarce and thus of great value*.

Choosing Our Destiny

In the coming years, we must choose our destiny as a nation. If we choose the existing system, the status quo and everything that is dependent on it will collapse once it encounters non-linear upheaval. The essence of non-linear dynamics is that small events can trigger monumental cascades of disruption. This will be our fate if we cling to our intrinsically corrupt and unsustainable status quo.

I have stressed the causal connection between scarcity and value, and the difference between force and power. Force is necessary to enforce the artificial scarcities and monopolies of corporations and the state. But force isn't power; *force is the absence of power*, for power attracts cooperation, effort and sacrifice because it benefits participants serving the common good.

In the status quo, the *illusion of choice* masks the reality that we're not given the option of an adaptable, resilient, sustainable system, because this option would fatally undermine the status quo.

People naturally value what's scarce and beneficial. What's scarce are *social constructs that optimize adaptability and resilience*, and systems that generate these dynamics as their only possible output.

Nation-states that rely on force, inequality, neofeudalism, squandering resources and the infinite expansion of consumption and debt are doomed to collapse. A great many nations have social constructs that serve the interests of the few at the expense of the many. The social constructs of the status quo are abundant and thus of little value.

Nation-states that institutionalize social constructs that optimize adaptability and offer equal opportunities for agency and accumulating capital will attract capital, talent and participants willing to contribute to the common good and make sacrifices on behalf of the system that offers everyone value and opportunity.

This all sounds abstract, so let's compare the future of a typical individual a decade hence in each system.

If the current status quo still holds sway, the individual will be reduced to dependent peonage on the state's Universal Basic Income, a stipend that is losing purchasing power, leaving fewer options for the recipient and near-zero opportunity to accumulate meaningful capital. The individual has no agency in the political oligarchy or in the economy dominated by concentrated wealth and power. His role is to consume whatever he can after paying the interest and principle on his ever-rising debt. There is no shared purpose or meaningful participation in social constructs that serve the common good because the common good is defined as maximizing personal gain.

There is nothing to wake up and be excited about doing because the individual has no positive social role or opportunity to contribute or be needed. He is superfluous and he knows it. His options for employment are limited to commoditized BS work everyone knows has little value. The barriers to starting a formal business are so high that few can manage it, and the informal black market is fraught with the risk of crossing a heavy-handed authoritarian state and paying the resulting penalty.

Since expansion of consumption and credit is the one shared goal of the global economy, necessities have become scarce and the planet's natural economy has been strip-mined by those maximizing private gain by whatever means available. The tools of technology are owned by corporations and serve the corporate ontology of maximizing profits, an artificial scarcity enforced by the oligarchic pay-to-play state. The rich have become immeasurably richer and the powerful hold even more power, as there is no other possible output generated by the status quo's structure.

In the background, the corporate-controlled media issues a ceaseless stream of propaganda that euphorically promotes the ever-expanding Gross Domestic Product and other financial measures of growth, measures that ignore the decline in well-being and social mobility and the absence of social constructs that address local scarcities and social demand. Since the system has no means of recognizing such scarcities, communities have rotted on the vine. The only exceptions are the gated, guarded compounds of the wealthy.

Let's contrast this with the alternative future, where this same individual has a reason to get up in the morning: he's needed, and he's valued. He is a member of a community group he chose to belong to, engaged in a variety of projects addressing local scarcities, and he's paid for his labor by the group. He serves on the project committee, having been elected by his peers to serve. He's proud of the projects the group has completed and of what he's learned about management and working with others. He's acquired intellectual capital (skills) and social capital, as the group trades information, goods and services with other groups.

The group is self-funding the construction of new housing, a project he feels will better his own housing options. He's saving money and lending it to the new housing project at a fair rate of return.

He's free to start his own enterprise if he chooses to. The network of community groups thrives on a variety of talents, sources of goods and services, and this competition fuels improvements in efficiency and best practices. He's free to join another group (or groups) or even start a new group if he feels there's an unmet need a new group could address.

The benefits of the dynamic efforts of local groups are visible to everyone in the community, and the community has a vibrant sense of shared purpose. People may disagree on priorities and processes, but this is a healthy manifestation of adaptability and resilience.

Those who choose not to participate don't reap the rewards of contributing. Despite the endless complaints about something or other—the human condition—most people choose to participate because they miss the camaraderie, pay, purpose and sense of accomplishment when they stay at home.

Much of what was once shipped in via long supply chains from distant locales is now fabricated locally, and efforts to increase well-being using fewer resources are embedded in the system's incentives and guidelines. The group is equally networked to the world and other local groups, but as an independent node in a cooperative network.

As I write this in 2018, the cracks in the existing system are small. It's still easy to dismiss them as inconsequential. There is no pressing need to look at alternative structures.

This complacency will dissipate once the foundation cracks and efforts to sustain the status quo only widen the cracks. No one can predict the timeline of decay and collapse, but we can be confident that these are the only possible outputs of the status quo.

We have the tools to create a social construct that serves the many instead of the few, one that is sustainable on a finite planet, one that measures well-being not in terms of expansion of consumption but in the shared wealth of social demands being met for the benefit of all.

Charles Hugh Smith

November 2018
Berkeley, California
Hilo, Hawaii

Made in the USA
San Bernardino, CA
26 January 2019